Online Impulse Buying and Cognitive Dissonance

Giovanni Mattia • Alessio Di Leo
Ludovica Principato

Online Impulse Buying and Cognitive Dissonance

Examining the Effect of Mood on Consumer Behaviour

Giovanni Mattia
Department of Business Studies
Roma Tre University
Rome, Italy

Alessio Di Leo
Department of Business Studies and
Social Research
La Sapienza University
Rome, Italy

Ludovica Principato
Department of Business Studies
Roma Tre University
Rome, Italy

ISBN 978-3-030-65922-6   ISBN 978-3-030-65923-3   (eBook)
https://doi.org/10.1007/978-3-030-65923-3

© The Author(s), under exclusive licence to Springer Nature Switzerland AG 2021
This work is subject to copyright. All rights are solely and exclusively licensed by the Publisher, whether the whole or part of the material is concerned, specifically the rights of translation, reprinting, reuse of illustrations, recitation, broadcasting, reproduction on microfilms or in any other physical way, and transmission or information storage and retrieval, electronic adaptation, computer software, or by similar or dissimilar methodology now known or hereafter developed.
The use of general descriptive names, registered names, trademarks, service marks, etc. in this publication does not imply, even in the absence of a specific statement, that such names are exempt from the relevant protective laws and regulations and therefore free for general use.
The publisher, the authors and the editors are safe to assume that the advice and information in this book are believed to be true and accurate at the date of publication. Neither the publisher nor the authors or the editors give a warranty, expressed or implied, with respect to the material contained herein or for any errors or omissions that may have been made. The publisher remains neutral with regard to jurisdictional claims in published maps and institutional affiliations.

Cover pattern © Melisa Hasan

This Palgrave Macmillan imprint is published by the registered company Springer Nature Switzerland AG.
The registered company address is: Gewerbestrasse 11, 6330 Cham, Switzerland

ACKNOWLEDGMENTS

The authors would like to acknowledge the valuable contribution of Dr. Dario Cherubini for the first draft of chapters 2–5 and the initial assessment of the conceptual framework of the present study, and Dr. Chiara Pugliese for her comprehensive review of technology acceptance models.

CONTENTS

1	**Introduction**	1
2	**The Impulse Buying**	5
	References	10
3	**The Cognitive Dissonance**	13
	References	21
4	**The Affect State**	25
	References	28
5	**Measuring the Constructs of Impulse Buying, Cognitive Dissonance, and Affect State**	31
	The Impulse Buying Tendency Scale (IBTS)	32
	The Sweeney Scale	33
	The PANAS Scale	34
	References	35
6	**On-line Consumer Behavior and Technology Acceptance Models**	37
	References	44

viii CONTENTS

7 Drivers for On-line Impulse Purchases of Highly Symbolic Products 47
References 51

8 PC-based Versus Mobile-Based On-line Shopping 55
References 58

9 Millennials and On-line Shopping: The Case of Smartphones 61
References 67

10 The Study 71
Introduction 71
Theoretical Background and Hypothesis 72
Methodology 74
Results and Discussion 75
Conclusion 76
References 79

References 81

LIST OF FIGURES

Fig. 3.1   Cognitive dissonance visual representation. (Source: Author's
elaboration)   14
Fig. 10.1   Conceptual model. (Source: Author's elaboration)   74

List of Tables

Table 9.1	Intergenerational differences	62
Table 10.1	Research steps	74
Table 10.2	Sample demographics	75

CHAPTER 1

Introduction

Abstract In this chapter a summary of the book content is presented. An overall recognition of impulse buying under positive affect state and cognitive dissonance is explained, coupled with the conceptual framework which gave rise to the study in the last section of the book. In particular, it is highlighted that smartphone was chosen as the highly symbolic product subject to an impulse purchase, that the purchase takes place through an e-retailing channel via desktop personal computer, and that the considered target of purchasers is represented by Millennials.

Keywords Impulse buying • Cognitive dissonance • Positive affect state • Online commerce • Millennials

Consumers' beliefs and attitudes toward on-line sales significantly influence their buying behavior on the internet. However, the impact of these thoughts and beliefs on the decision to make an on-line purchase is not direct, but is moderated by a crucial factor, namely the emotions experienced while browsing an e-commerce website.

All the stimuli that consumers encounter and perceive, consciously or not, provoke reactions. When consumers look at a shop window or enter a point of sale, as well as when they open a website, the "objects" they see bring out in their mind thoughts and evaluations (e.g., they may think that prices are too high for the items in a clothing store, or that the shop

© The Author(s), under exclusive license to Springer Nature Switzerland AG 2021

G. Mattia et al., *Online Impulse Buying and Cognitive Dissonance*, https://doi.org/10.1007/978-3-030-65923-3_1

1

window is not set up in the right way, or that a webpage is confusing and difficult to navigate), but also generate a series of emotions. All these elements combine and create a "mix" that determines, in the end, the overall judgment of consumer experience.

If we consider different types of purchases, then the cognitive and affective components take on a different weight in orienting consumers' choices. These assessments differ depending on the product. On the one hand, for hedonistic products, we might suppose that consumers plan their eventual purchase in advance (when, where, and how much they want to spend), evaluating the alternatives available on the market as accurately as possible (e.g., visiting different points of sale, comparing models and prices, asking for advice from friends and acquaintances). On the other hand, for other products, the purchase decision can also be "improvised": a girl sees a pair of shoes in the window of a store, and "they must be hers", then she enters the store and purchases them.

Impulse buying is a well-known topic in marketing, so well-known that it has been talked about for decades and companies try to encourage it, being a good source of revenues. Impulse buying can be considered a behavior almost physiologically connected to human nature. However, the personality traits that trigger an impulse purchase are different: there are in fact more predisposed subjects than others. In the end, however, no one can say to be totally indifferent from this practice.

Impulse buying depends on situations, as well as on the type of product. For example, the store, physical or virtual, can affect the "carefreeness" of a choice. Just think of the flagship stores, designed to create a consumer immersion into the brand experience, or a particularly stimulating e-shopping platform, perhaps consulted through the smartphone, which pushes to an easy click on the cart.

Of course, it is not just context that matters. Certain products, usually those of modest value, make us better falling into the trap of impulsiveness. In this case, the low involvement in the purchase dictates the speed of the decision. However, the concept of modest value is relative, being linked to the economic availability of each one. But even products that seem to require more reflection, if only for their higher price, fall among the impulse purchases: a cutting-edge laptop, or a holiday in an exclusive place can be both included among them, but in this case the decision-making process must be sought in symbolic (such as the image of a brand) and hedonistic components of which they are bearers.

Sometimes, however, it can happen that once a consumer comes back home, or after having received the item ordered on-line, it may raise regret toward the purchase. The product (or service) is not exactly as one thought and not worth the money spent, or, more simply, unnecessary. Then, in the throes of this anxiety of failure, people are looking for reasons—more or less robust, more or less logical—to justify the choices made.

Consumer behavior scholars and psychologists call this self-convincing operation cognitive dissonance. As in the case of impulse buying, certain individuals are more sensitive than others to develop the state of dissonance, so it is always necessary to avoid generalizations: repentance is around the corner, but it is not automatic.

The sense of frustration that cognitive dissonance produces is also a point of interest for marketers, who wonder how to neutralize it, or at least reduce it, because in case of success the situation of discomfort is replaced by relief, which tends to be more easily memorized up to become an antecedent of future repeated purchases.

Many attempts have been made by companies under this respect: creating an enjoyable shopping experience, increasing product involvement, and so on.

One point, however, remains still not answered. What will happen if the consumer accomplishes an impulse buying while experiencing a positive affect state? Is a positive mood able to reduce the unleashing of the cognitive dissonance?

This work aims to understand how impulse buying can lead to the onset of cognitive dissonance. The objective of the research is to measure whether the effect of a positive affect state at the moment of an impulse purchase can moderate, positively or negatively, the occurrence of cognitive dissonance. The context of the experiment concerns a product with a strong expressive value as the smartphone, within the target of the Millennials, who are familiar with technology and have a propensity to hedonic purchases. Another aspect of restriction of the research perimeter is the channel adopted to finalize the impulsive transaction, that is, on-line shopping using a pc-desktop.

It is appropriate to briefly contextualize the reasons that led to the decision to investigate in this area. First of all, impulse buying, especially for products with an expressive component, is able to involve, at different times and circumstances, all consumers. Second, the cognitive dissonance, being a consequence of impulse buying, is extensively studied in literature, as its dystonic effects may depress consumer's future purchase intention.

Therefore, it requires reduction actions that companies should implement to maintain a profitable relationship. Third, we have considered the role of moderation of the positive affect state on the purchase, whose effects, so far, have not been treated in much detail from researchers. In fact, numerous studies, which will be discussed in the following chapters, recognize the positive affect state as an antecedent that modulates the propensity to the impulse buying. On the contrary, to the best of our knowledge, there are no contributions evaluating the impact of the positive affect state on the onset of cognitive dissonance. This aspect is particularly relevant: if the hypothesis of influence on cognitive dissonance was empirically demonstrated, companies could prepare situational conditions—especially environmental ones—to proactively intervene before cognitive dissonance occurs. It cannot be excluded, and this aspect should be placed among the possible future developments of research, which even the negative affective state could affect cognitive dissonance. However, it has been chosen to limit the scope of the study to the positive affect state, assuming as more likely the ability of this condition to exert an impact of the reduction of cognitive dissonance compared to the negative one.

Some additional conditions of the analysis have been placed: (1) the choice of the smartphone as a reference product, characterized by an unquestionable expressive value, whose diffusion has led to the construction of a brand-oriented offer system, and an emotional effect able to solicit a more impulsive choice; (2) the target of Millennials, who massively use smartphone; (3) the choice of on-line shopping based on pc instead of mobile, to eliminate the most impulsive part that the mobile phone can produce thanks to its instantaneousness.

In the following chapters, the individual components of the analysis structure will be examined in-depth, concluding with the results of an empirical research aimed at verifying the hypothesis previously exposed.

CHAPTER 2

The Impulse Buying

Abstract A theoretical background of impulse buying is the core of this chapter. After its definition, a differentiation among compulsive buying and unplanned purchasing is carried out. Subsequently, conditions which drive impulse buying and its connection with the personality traits and situational dimensions are examined. Furthermore, a comparison among impulse buying, cultures, and socio-demographic factors are considered. The impact of technology in boosting impulsive buying constitutes the final part of the chapter.

Keywords Impulse buying • Compulsive buying • Unplanned purchase • Personality traits • Situational dimension • Socio-demographic factors • Technology

Consumers do not always plan their purchases, as they deal with three types of buying alternatives: thoroughly planned, partially planned, and unplanned (Troilo 2015; Blackwell et al. 2012).

Impulsiveness is defined as "a strong, sometimes irresistible stimulus; a sudden inclination to act without deliberation" (Goldenson 1984). It can, therefore, represent an uncontrollable impulse, which coincides with a lack of concern for objective reasoning (Bellman 2012). Several studies involving either the academic or the professional field highlighted that

© The Author(s), under exclusive license to Springer Nature
Switzerland AG 2021
G. Mattia et al., *Online Impulse Buying and Cognitive Dissonance*,
https://doi.org/10.1007/978-3-030-65923-3_2

from 40 to 80% of total purchases can be attributable to the impulse behavior, depending on the type of product (Amos et al. 2014).

Stern (1962) offered an exhaustive classification of impulse buying, distinguishing four different types: (1) pure impulse buying, which refers to the radical breaking of the normal buying pattern—it happens when the consumer has no intention to buy, but the emotions aroused by the product lead him/her to accomplish a purchase; (2) impulse buying, emerging when consumer, while seeing a product, thinks, for example, that his personal stock is low, or alternatively recalls an advertisement, an information about the product, or simply a previous desire to buy it; (3) unplanned impulse purchase, which occurs when the consumer sees a product for the first time and discovers a need that it can satisfy; (4) planned impulse purchase, happening when the consumer is keen on buying certain products, depending on special offers and in-store promotions.

Rook's contribution (1987) had a significant impact on the conceptualization of the impulse buying definition. According to the author, in fact, "[…] impulse buying occurs when a consumer experiences a sudden, often powerful, and persistent desire to buy something immediately".

Following Stern classification, other authors engaged in further taxonomies. Chang et al. (2014) define three types of products that fall within impulse buying (unplanned, purchased for a sudden impulse, and purchased for the excitement of research), while other researchers set different indicators to measure impulse buying (something not on the shopping list or something unplanned, purchased by a person considering the fun to buy, but not considering the consequences) (Mohan et al. 2013).

Over the years, the phenomenon of impulsiveness has been explored by different disciplines (psychology, sociology, philosophy, etc.). In the context of consumer behavior, all the above types of impulse purchase gained the attention of the academic literature. However, an additional aspect of the impulse buying deserves to be brought to the attention: it is a direct consequence of a so-called spot need. The sight of a product is reminiscent of a need, which triggers a real desire, which in turn culminates in purchase to satisfy an immediate consumption (Simonson 1990). In this regard, several authors (Amos et al. 2014; Sharma et al. 2010; Luna and Quintanilla 2000) have extended the concept, establishing that impulse buying emerges after a consumer is exposed to a stimulus. The impulse purchase is, therefore, a purchase stimulated by the moment in which it happens (Kacen and Lee 2002).

Impulse purchase should be distinguished from compulsive one. The former can be described as the urgency to purchase something, mainly as a result of proximity to the object (Rook and Fisher 1995). The latter is described as the effect of chronic behavior in response to negative feelings or events (O'Guinn and Faber 1989). An important difference between the two typologies lies in the motivation: in the first case, it is based more on the positive effects of the purchase, especially gratification and attraction toward the product (Hoch and Lowenstein 1991). In the second, instead, it is more functional in calming negative emotions and, therefore, unrelated to the object (O'Guinn and Faber 1989). In fact, impulse buying is activated by emotional stimuli and implies a temptation difficult to resist, whereas compulsive buying refers to a dysfunctional and repetitive urgency to buy. It represents therefore a psychological disorder, which implies any lack of behavioral control (Babin and Harris 2013; Flight et al. 2012).

Impulse purchases must also be distinguished from unplanned purchases. It can be said that impulse purchases are always unplanned, whereas the unplanned purchases are not always impulsive (Koski 2004). An unplanned purchase takes place when consumers need to purchase a product not included in their shopping list. What differentiates them from impulse purchases is the absence of an urgent desire or strong positive feelings felt in-store, physical or virtual (Amos et al. 2014).

A study by Luna and Quintanilla (2000) showed that impulse buying is mainly affected by an emotional nature and that hedonistic aspects determine consumer behavior. Coherently, Sharma et al. (2010) defined impulse buying as a sudden, compelling desire with hedonistically complex roots, in which the speed of impulsive decision prevents from realizing any thought, evaluation of alternatives, or possible implications occurring in the future. Accordingly, impulse buyers are more driven by emotions and do not reflect on information and alternatives of choice (Cobb and Hoyer 1986).

Impulse buying is considered as a three-phase process: (1) the antecedent step, (2) the trigger step, and (3) the act of buying (Sundström et al. 2013). The first phase concerns personality traits, socio-cultural factors, beliefs, and values. The second refers to stimuli deriving from the environment and the interaction between consumers. The third concerns the decision-making process and the act of purchase. Pirog and Roberts (2007) have shown that the consequences of impulse buying, including the perception of guilt and regret resulting from unnecessary expenditure, require more reassurance to justify the decisions taken, precisely in light of the fact that pre-purchase actions (e.g., information seeking) are not entirely rational (Eiser 1990).

Studies in the field of impulsivity postulate that in the pre-purchase phase consumers are more responsive to their feelings and moods, but that surrendering to impulse buying inclinations can be decisive in affecting a certain psychological vulnerability in the post-purchase phase (Rook 1987). Given the characteristics that distinguish most purchasing decision-making processes, O'Guinn and Faber (1989) observed how impulse purchasers often perceive consumption as an activity of self-completion, or a sort of personal gratification. On the contrary, Bayley and Nancarrow (1998) argued that impulse buying does not exclude a process of identifying and selecting alternatives, at least in certain situations, while pursuing the satisfaction of hedonistic motivations.

Amos et al. (2014) identified both internal factors, related to personal traits and psychology, and external ones, referred to situational characteristics such as store and product, which taken together influence the impulse to buy. Two factors emerged as particularly important in impulse buying behavior: (1) the emotions of individuals and (2) the culture in which they live. The impulse buyer is a much more emotional consumer than the non-impulse one and is influenced by the state of mind he/she presents at the moment of purchase, without thinking about post-purchase phase (Weinberg and Gottwald 1982).

Regarding cultural differences, there are no significant differences in purchasing impulsiveness between Asians and Caucasians (Kacen and Lee 2002). On the contrary, the more Caucasians adopt the so-called independence concept, the more they tend to behave impulsively during their purchases. Moreover, while the age factor does not seem relevant for Caucasians, it becomes relevant for Asians, who will purchase less impulsively with the growing of age (Kacen and Lee 2002).

Demographic characteristics constitute a further, significant behavioral difference. In this regard, the literature has highlighted the different impulse buying behavior with respect to gender and age. As far as gender is concerned, women are more inclined to impulse buying than males, as well as impulse product choices (Verplanken and Herabadi 2001; Dittmar et al. 1995), while age is a factor that influences the quantity of products impulsively purchased and is mostly related to some specific groups, such as those under 35 years of age (Bellenger et al. 1978).

The theme related to the economic availability has to be considered equally. In fact, there can be a corresponding increase in purchases, including unplanned purchases (Tifferet and Herstein 2012), when economic availability grows.

Alongside psychological and demographic characteristics, situational factors have also to be taken into account as an antecedent category of impulse buying. Situational antecedents can be considered as external stimuli which provoke the urgency to buy—given a positive tendency to act on an impulse basis—such as those related to the shopping environment or, more generally, to marketing activities of the companies. In addition, time and financial constraints equally act as external drivers of impulse buying, as they can limit or rather expand the willingness to put in place an impulse purchase (Sharma et al. 2010; Dholakia 2000).

With the advancement of technology and its global adoption, the market has undergone regular changes in its structure. According to Iram and Chacharkar (2017), it is possible to identify a tight connection between technology and the phenomenon of impulse buying. For the authors, consumer behavior is the result of new and constantly improved purchasing methods, such as the adoption of various digital platforms. They argued that consumptions to some extent attributable to the impulsiveness tend to be oriented toward emotional choices and are influenced by cultural characteristics. The large number of products and services very often evaluated at the same time, to which the consumer is exposed, creates fertile ground for impulsive buying opportunities. In fact, it is estimated, just to name a few, that 60% of in-store purchases are not planned (Dialogica 2017) and that in the United States about 5400 euros per year per person are devoted to this kind of purchases (Slickdeals 2018).

Studies on impulsive behavior have found an application in marketing strategies since impulse buying is an extension of the natural behavior of a human being (Rook 1987). Marketing strategies take advantage of the potential effect of an environment designed to provide stimuli for impulse and unplanned purchasing. In this regard, Iram and Chacharkar (2017) provided an overview of marketing factors that entice consumers to make an impulse or unplanned purchase: (1) advertising: marketing succeeds in reaching target consumers through numerous channels and touch points, which can influence purchasing behavior, as well as the culture of a country; (2) promotions: various forms of discount on a product can guide the purchase decision. The famous claim "buy-one-take-two" gives the consumer a feeling of satisfaction finding the right offer and getting the right deal; (3) sales staff: salespeople prepared to leverage customer's emotions and stimulate them can guide decision-making process; (4) product positioning in-store: display techniques can lead to increase the impulse buying; (5) time pressure: the increased time spent at the point of sale is related to the possibility of impulse buying (Iyer 1989).

REFERENCES

Amos, C., Holmes, G. R., & Keneson, W. C. (2014). A meta-analysis of consumer impulse buying. Journal of Retailing and Consumer Services, Vol. 21, No. 2, pp. 86–97.

Babin, B., & Harris, E., 2013. CB5. South-Western, Mason, OH.

Bayley, G., & Nancarrow, C. (1998). Impulse purchasing: a qualitative exploration of the phenomenon. Qualitative Market Research: An International Journal. Vol. 1, No. 2, pp. 99–114.

Bellenger, D. N., Robertson, D. H., & Hirschman, E. C. (1978). Impulse buying varies by product. Journal of Advertising Research, Vol. 18, No. 6, pp. 15–18.

Bellman, S. B. (2012). I would rather be happy than right: consumer impulsivity, risky decision making, and accountability. PhD (Doctor of Philosophy) thesis, University of Iowa.

Blackwell, R. D., Miniard, P.-W., & Engel, J. F. (2012). Consumer behavior. 9th edition, Cengage Learning, Asia.

Chang, H. J., Yan, R. N., & Eckman, M. (2014). Moderating effects of situational characteristics on impulse buying. International Journal of Retail & Distribution Management, Vol. 42, No. 4, pp. 298–314.

Cobb, C. J., & Hoyer, W. D. (1986). Planned versus impulse purchase behavior. Journal of Retailing. Vol. 62, No. 4, pp. 384–409.

Dholakia, U. M. (2000). Temptation and resistance: an integrated model of consumption impulse. Psychol. Mark., 17 (11), 955–982.

Dialogica (2017). Spesa programmata o impulso? I dati di una ricerca. http://dialogica.it/blog/2017/10/26/spesa-programmata-o-impulso-i-dati-di-una-ricerca [Last accessed: June 16, 2020].

Dittmar, H., Beattie, J., & Friese, S. (1995). Gender identity and material symbols: Objects and decision considerations in impulse purchases. Journal of Economic Psychology, Vol. 16, No. 3, pp. 491–511.

Eiser, C. (1990). Psychological effects of chronic disease. Journal of Child Psychology and Psychiatry, Vol. 31, No. 1, pp. 85–98.

Flight, R., Roundtree, M., & Beatty, S. (2012). Feeling the urge: Affect in impulsive and compulsive buying. Journal of Marketing Theory and Practice, Vol. 20, Issue 4, 453–466.

Goldenson, R. M. (1984). Longman Dictionary of Psychology and Psychiatry, Kaplan Publishing.

Hoch, S. J., & Lowenstein, G. F. (1991). Time-inconsistent preferences and consumer self-control. Journal of Consumer Research, Vol. 17, pp. 492–507.

Iram, M., & Chacharkar, D. Y. (2017). Model of impulse buying behavior. BVIMSR's Journal of Management Research, Vol. 9, No. 1, pp. 45–53.

Iyer, E. S. (1989). Unplanned purchasing: knowledge of shopping environment and Time Pressure. Journal of Retailing, Vol. 65, No. 1, 40–58.

Kacen, J. J., & Lee, J. A. (2002). The influence of culture on consumer impulsive buying behavior. Journal of Consumer Psychology, Vol. 12, No. 2, pp. 163–176.

Koski, N. (2004). Impulse buying on the internet: encouraging and discouraging factors. Frontiers of E-business Research, Vol. 4, pp. 23–35.

Luna, R., & Quintanilla, I. (2000). El modelo de compra ACB. Una nueva conceptualizacion de la compra por impulso. Esic Market. Revista Internacional de Economía y Empresa, Vol. 106, No.1, pp. 151–163.

Mohan, G., Sharina, P., & Sivakumaran, B. (2013). Impact of store environment on impulse buying behavior. European Journal of Marketing, Vol. 47, No. 10, pp. 1711–1732.

O'Guinn, T. C., & Faber, R. J. (1989). Compulsive buying: a phenomenological exploration. Journal of Consumer Research, Vol. 16, pp. 147–157.

Pirog, S. F., & Roberts, J. A. (2007). Personality and credit card misuse among college students: the mediating role of impulsiveness. Journal of Marketing Theory and Practice, Vol. 15, No. 1, pp. 65–77.

Rook, D. W. (1987). The Buying Impulse. Journal of Consumer Research, Vol. 14, No. 2, pp. 189–197.

Rook, D. W., & Fisher, R. J. (1995). Normative influences on impulsive buying behavior. Journal of Consumer Research, Vol. 22, No. 3, pp. 305–313.

Sharma, P., Sivakumaran, B., & Marshall, R. (2010). Exploring impulse buying and variety seeking by retail shoppers: towards a common conceptual framework. Journal of Marketing Management, Vol. 26, No. 5–6, pp. 473–494.

Simonson, I. (1990). The effect of purchase quantity and timing on variety-seeking behavior. Journal of Marketing Research, Vol. 27, No. 2, pp. 150–162.

Slickdeals (2018). Slickdeals shares new survey data showing Americans spend $324,000 on impulse buys in their lifetime. https://slickdeals.net/forums/forumdisplay.php?f=39 [Last accessed: June 16, 2020].

Stern, H. (1962). The significance of impulse buying today. Journal of Marketing, Vol. 26, No. 2, pp. 59–62.

Sundström, M., Balkow, J., Florhed, J., Tjernström, M., & Wadenfors, P. (2013). Inpulsive buying behaviour: the role of feelings when shopping for on-line fashion. In: 17th European association for education and research in commercial distribution.

Tifferet, S., & Herstein, R. (2012). Gender differences in brand commitment, impulse buying, and hedonic consumption. Journal of Product & Brand Management., Vol. 21, No. 3, pp. 176–182.

Troilo, G. (2015). Marketing in creative industries: value, experience and creativity. Macmillan International Higher Education.

Verplanken, B., & Herabadi, A. (2001). Individual differences in impulse buying tendency: feeling and no thinking. European Journal of Personality, Vol. 15(S1), pp. S71–S83.

Weinberg, P., & Gottwald, W. (1982). Impulsive consumer buying as a result of emotions. Journal of Business Research, Vol. 10, No. 1, pp. 43–57.

CHAPTER 3

The Cognitive Dissonance

Abstract As for the previous one, aim of the present chapter is to offer a comprehensive theoretical framework of cognitive dissonance. After the definition offered by Festinger, the founder of cognitive dissonance theory, at first the context of cognitive dissonance is examined, which mainly refer to the involvement toward the product and the lack of control on the purchasing process, and gives rise to a state of discomfort. Strategies which companies can put in place to help consumers reduce the adverse state of cognitive dissonance are proposed in the final part of the chapter.

Keywords Cognitive dissonance • Anxiety • Involvement • Decision control • Discomfort • Reduction strategies

To satisfy needs, consumers tend to use their cognitive abilities to achieve the best possible level of satisfaction. Although the intention is to rationalize their purchasing decisions, they will often find themselves in a situation of doubt, wondering to what extent their decisions are correct. The most common behavior is to compare the purchase made with the myriad of alternatives on the market (Simpson and Willer 2008). The individual will ask himself whether buying that product makes sense and why is he pervaded by a sense of dissatisfaction, regret, and psychological pain (Fig. 3.1).

Chang and Tseng (2014) explained that impulse shoppers experience post-purchase anxiety when compared with doubts about their choice,

© The Author(s), under exclusive license to Springer Nature Switzerland AG 2021
G. Mattia et al., *Online Impulse Buying and Cognitive Dissonance*, https://doi.org/10.1007/978-3-030-65923-3_3

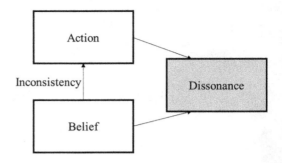

Fig. 3.1 Cognitive dissonance visual representation. (Source: Author's elaboration)

perhaps recognizing undesirable characteristics they had previously ignored. The consequences of unplanned purchases can lead to the development of a psychological discomfort or cognitive dissonance. The process of cognitive dissonance takes place in four phases: (1) inconsistency between cognitions, (2) state of dissonance, (3) reduction strategy, and (4) relief from dissonance (Devine et al. 1994).

According to Festinger's theory (1957), cognition is defined as every element of the personality, including attitudes, emotions, beliefs, and behaviors. Cognitions that contradict consumer perceptions are defined as dissonant. Coherent cognitions are instead referred to as consonants. Many years later, after evolving his theory, Festinger (1985) defined cognitive dissonance as "an uncomfortable tension resulting from having two conflicting thoughts at the same time, or the implementation of behavior with one or more beliefs deeply rooted in the individual". Dissonance theory (Festinger 1985) provided to be particularly suitable in understanding how consumers, under specific conditions, will seek out or avoid information. However, according to recent research (Mills 2019; Beauvois and Joule 2019) dissonance is determined by desired consequences and importance of cognitions. Coherenlty, Harmon-Jones (2019) underlined that dissonance plays a prominent role in many information searching processing, as well as connections between dissonance and other motivational processes.

A consumer capable of activating ideas and behaviors consistent with each other gives rise to the phenomenon of cognitive consonance, and its result is a satisfying emotional situation. Cognitive dissonance, instead, has its origin in the inconsistency between what the individual thinks and how he behaves.

As for impulse buying, the theory of cognitive dissonance has generated great interest and has been explored in a multitude of domains, including psychology and marketing. According to a large part of the literature (Sweeney and Chew 2000; Oliver 1997; Mowen and Minor 1995; Korgaonkar and Moschis 1982; Cummings and Venkatesan 1976), there are three main conditions thanks to which a purchase can favor the growth of cognitive dissonance:

- The purchase decision must be crucial for the consumer, for example, when it involves a very high price being paid, or a "psychological cost".
- The consumer is free to choose among various alternatives.
- The purchase decision is hardly reversible, and the consumer feels the victim of the circumstances.

The third condition refers to the consumer feeling of not being the master of the final decision, given that the choice is influenced by external factors. This situation creates a psychological inconsistency and will generate a state of strain that the consumer will try to resolve as quickly as possible. One way to deal with the problem is usually to choose the shortest way and the least cognitive effort, for example, by concluding that the seller has deceived in the purchase. This allows the consumer not to destroy his basic belief, alleviating his state of discomfort without wondering too much about the truthfulness of the conclusion he reached.

What just stated above shows how contradictory convictions create uncomfortable situation in consumers, who activate a process of mental recovery (Babu and Manoj 2009) leading to:

- Search for information that supports the sustained belief.
- Change the beliefs given the new condition.

Despite the adjective "cognitive", the phenomenon of dissonance presents a preponderant emotional dimension (Elliot and Devine 1994) and can reasonably occur in the post-purchase, pre-purchase, and even pre-decisional phases (Koller and Salzberger 2007). In contrast to the thesis supported by Festinger, which conceived the reduction of the dissonance in a rational way, the process could instead lead to a form of "self-deception" and, in this case, the emotional factors, of which the consumer is unaware, nurture the process itself (Zanna and Cooper 1974).

The relationship between impulse buying and cognitive dissonance has been the subject of intense debate within the scientific community. On the one hand, studies conducted by Bayley and Nancarrow (1998) found a negative relationship between the two phenomena, concluding that consumers tend to make unplanned purchases to reduce discomfort, due to previous situations of cognitive dissonance. Other studies from authors such as Wood (2005) found a positive relationship between impulsive buying and cognitive dissonance. The most recent research agrees that impulse buying leads to greater cognitive dissonance than the planned purchases (Deutsch and Strack 2008). Finally, Xiao and Nicholson (2013) theorized a positive relationship between impulse purchases and cognitive dissonance, arguing that the two phenomena are directly proportional.

According to the reflective-impulsive model (RIM), lack of self-control often comes first an impulsive behavior. Consequently, it is conceivable that this type of situation may continue even after the purchase, so a low level of self-control during a phase of repentance and reflection could lead to stronger occurrences of cognitive dissonance. From this point of view, individuals characterized by a trait of impulsivity are more likely to be exposed to the onset of cognitive dissonance (Deutsch et al. 2016). Hence, a great tendency to unplanned purchases tends to be followed by high cognitive dissonance. Currently, the latter represents a majority position in the literature.

The self-standards model by Stone and Cooper (2001) offers three main reasons which give rise to the need of reducing the cognitive dissonance: (1) self-affirmation, (2) self-consistency, and (3) way of being. These concepts highlight how cognitive dissonance is inextricably linked not only to the opinion of others, but, above all, to what consumers think about themselves. Each consumer evaluates products differently depending on his/her specific personal beliefs. Many of these are more concerned with the quality of the product and associated with a given brand, but in addition, also the affective variables, that is, the pleasant emotions aroused by the product, the packaging, or the point of sale, have to be considered (Godin 2018).

Most purchasing decisions involve dissonant feelings, as consumers increasingly tend to make comparisons among different products and brands (Pepels 2005). For instance, should a selected product be similar to other alternatives on the market, it will be easier to be "victim" of cognitive dissonance, while if the product is perceived as unique, the more difficult it will be. Imagine a potential buyer considering the purchase of laptop computer and assume that his decisions depend on the comparison between two different models. Each alternative has combinations of desirable (or rejectable) features, such as high speed, but poor memory, or high video quality, but little usability. The consumer will almost certainly be caused to select the combination that, at the time of choice, will be deemed more satisfactory. Despite this, since one of the two models is not superior to the other in all the characteristics, the more the rejected alternative will prove to be better than that chosen, the greater dissonance will be generated as a result of the decision taken (Harmon-Jones and Mills 1999). Post-decision cognitive dissonance arises from the fact that each of the alternatives evaluated by the consumer usually possesses both advantages and disadvantages. So, once the purchase decision has been made, the chosen alternative has some downsides not considered before, just as each of the discarded alternatives offers some attractive features (Losch and Cacioppo 1990).

In the late 1970s, the literature focused on the analysis of dissonance experienced by the individuals following the different stages of product diffusion. Connole et al. (1977) showed that innovators, that is, those who try a newly introduced product first, will seek more information attempting to reinforce the positive aspects of their choice much more than others. In the early 1980s, the focus of the research shifted to the level of the involvement with a product, and how it influences post-purchase evaluation, bringing to light that high expectations before purchase generate more favorable evaluations (Korgaonkar and Moschis 1982). Involvement depends on several factors: (1) the pleasure toward the product, (2) its symbolic value, (3) the importance of the risk connected to its purchase, and (4) the probability of the mistake in buying (Laurent and Kapferer 1985).

Therefore, it was suggested that high-involvement products should be designed following promotional mixes that evoke high expectations so that consumers would show less dissonance after purchase. In this regard, Holloway (1967) can be considered a pioneer, as he found that emotionally stimulated and positively involved consumers experienced less cognitive dissonance. In addition, consumers provided with adequate information were less likely to experience dissonance. The involvement of consumers with a product has been studied through the dimensions of intensity (strong or weak) and nature (cognitive or affective), that is, as a mix of the subject's psychological state between product type and purchasing situation (Stone et al. 2013). The intrinsic qualities of the product that feed the involvement are less significant than the way the individual perceives them (Knox and Inkster 1968). Consequently, consumers would prefer to buy products related to brands that are more compatible with their image (Churchilor and Peter 2003). In more general terms, highly involved individuals should be more inclined to stable positions in their knowledge and with a greater ability to manage decision making and subsequent risks (Venkatraman and Huettel 2012; Mittal 1989), while impulse buyers might be more risk-tolerant, tending to underestimate a disappointment of expectations; otherwise they would tend to plan more (Babu and Gallayanee 2010).

Continuing to deal with the relationship between cognitive dissonance and involvement, other studies (Zaichkowsky 1985) agree that impulse buying leads to a greater cognitive dissonance than that planned, according to the level of involvement. Such a condition refers to the amount of time, thought, energy, and other resources which people devote to the purchasing process (Beatty and Kahle 1988). Higher levels of involvement are linked to cognitive activity aimed at finding information and evaluating alternatives (Nunes and Drèze 2006). On the contrary, if a purchase is irrelevant, the individual tends to choose according to a marginal learning process, minimizing cognitive activities of all kinds.

More recently, Babu and Manoj (2009) pointed out that a good way to raise interest in the consumer is to identify its relationships with other involvement-related constructs, for example, their involvement during the purchase journey, in addition to the product itself. Behind every purchase, there is a different degree of involvement. Sometimes, due to complex interactions of situational factors, even routine purchases can present considerable levels of involvement (Beharrell and Denison 1995). Involvement and cognitive dissonance, considered motivational constructs, influence consumer behavior. Cognitive dissonance associated with high levels of involvement is much more difficult to cope, compared to that with a low level of involvement (Babu and Manoj 2009).

To reduce the post-purchase dissonance, consumers rely on three different approaches: (1) increase the attractiveness of the purchased brand/product, (2) decrease that of the rejected alternatives (Hawkins and Mothersbaugh 2010), (3) modify the reference scheme used to make the choice. In fact, the review of the product during the post-purchase phase in terms of advantages and disadvantages represents an innate response and is therefore linked to the phenomenon of cognitive dissonance, since it is extremely difficult to live with contradictory knowledge. In this case, the positive characteristics not owned by the chosen product/service are underestimated, whereas all those aspects on which the chosen alternative was superior are overestimated. For example, there will be less dissonance after choosing between two computers if one considers a distinction between the category of gaming computers and the category of work computers. In so doing, consumers aim to reduce the comparability between the two alternatives, thus limiting the onsetting of cognitive dissonance. In fact, the choice not to have bought computer A opting instead for computer B will find its justification in not belonging to the category certainly best suited to the needs of the buyer. This happens because the belief that consumers were forced by circumstances to make that type of purchase gives the opportunity to better justify the appropriateness of the choice made.

In any case, post-purchase behavior possesses a remarkable importance for marketing. In this phase, the consumer assesses whether he/she gains a sense of satisfaction in the product or service. When a negative state of mind occurs, that is, when there is a substantial difference between the expected and actual performance of a certain product or service (functional, emotional, and symbolic), this may also influence future choices, in the case of either planned or unplanned purchases (Iram and Chacharkar 2017). The cognitive pattern of consumers, the rules of their decision-making process, and individual and situational emotional differences, therefore, determine the establishment of cognitive dissonance. Under this respect, however, opposing positions can be found in the academic literature. Sofi and Najar (2018), for instance, argue that people with a higher degree of cognitive dissonance are more likely to approve a purchasing decision despite being irrational and illogical, in order to free themselves from the situation of inner conflict. Moreover, they report that it would be fair to think that this cognitive imbalance may lead the consumer to reflect on future decisions. On the contrary, the buyer presenting an impulse purchasing behavior tends not to engage in a deep reflection on the future consequences of an unthinking behavior, despite the negative emotions producing a high level of stress (Laird 2007). Consequently, it is not possible to say that the resolution of post-decision dissonance ensures that consumers tend to remind attitudes and behaviors causing the creation of cognitive dissonance. It is in fact extremely rare for people to reform their future attitude in contrast with their fundamental beliefs (Pittman 1975).

From a marketing perspective, one way to help consumers smoothing cognitive dissonance out is to offer strong guarantees to increase the effectiveness of the service and provide detailed brochures on how to use products correctly (Bawa and Kansal 2008). This process consists of alternative actions (Babu and Gallayanee 2010): (1) searching for information to support beliefs and convictions endangered by cognitive dissonance and (2) radically changing one's beliefs undermined by cognitive dissonance. Bearing in mind that cognitive dissonance can make the individual's perception significantly distorted, this is also a valuable clue for marketing professionals, especially when trying to study how the consumers develop a wrong view of the product or service (Balcetis and Dunning 2010).

Over time, extensive sociological and psychological studies on impulse buying behavior have moved toward the research for marketing strategies aimed at triggering a high customer loyalty. The fact that consumers proactively seek out messages containing information to support their choice prompts marketing managers to provide reinforcing inputs to the purchase. This is intended to build a positive attitude toward the brand and to cancel any cognitive dissonance resulting from consumers' fear of making the wrong choice (Hoyer et al. 2001). When the above situation takes place, the provided information helps consumers to more easily re-evaluate their choice; for example, think of those packages containing messages of congratulations, certainly irrelevant to the purchase decision that has already taken place, but able to provide a certain reassurance (Axsom 1989), or to follow up calls made to ensure that consumers are not experiencing problems (Felser 1997). It can be said that activity to reduce cognitive dissonance resides in after-sales branding and communication activities (Mayer 2005). Hence, the increased receptivity of consumers to the information communicated after their purchase improves the relationship with the brand and helps to generate satisfaction and loyalty (Hawkins and Mothersbaugh 2010). Indeed, in the absence of follow-up to avoid or reduce dissonance, consumers may be more likely to select different brands in the future (Foxall 2002). In this regard, however, conflicting results have been documented on the effect of providing post-purchase information because only the consumer would be able to reduce his or her negative awareness apart from changing his or her attitude (Chang and Tseng 2014).

References

Axsom, D. (1989). Cognitive dissonance and behavior change in psychotherapy. Journal of Personality and Social Psychology. Vol. 25, No. 3, pp. 234–252.

Babu, G., & Manoj, E. (2009). Cognitive Dissonance and Purchase Involvement in the Consumer Behavior Context. Journal of Marketing Management, Vol. 8, No. 3–4, pp. 7–24.

Babu, G., & Gallayanee Y. (2010). Impulse buying and cognitive dissonance: A study conducted among the spring break student shoppers. Young Consumers, Vol. 11, pp. 291–306.

Balcetis, E., & Dunning, D. (2010). Wishful seeing: more desired objects are seen as closer. Psychological Science, Vol. 21, No. 1, pp. 147–152.

Bawa, A., & Kansal, P. (2008). Cognitive dissonance and the marketing of services: Some Issues. Journal of Services Research, Vol. 8, No. 2, pp. 31–51.

Bayley, G., & Nancarrow, C. (1998). Impulse purchasing: a qualitative exploration of the phenomenon. Qualitative Market Research: An International Journal. Vol. 1, No. 2, pp. 99–114.

Beatty, S. E., & Kahle, L. R. (1988). Alternative hierarchies of the attitude-behavior relationship: the impact of brand commitment and habit. Journal of the Academy of Marketing Science, Vol. 16, No. 2, pp. 1–10.

Beauvois, J.-L., & Joule, R.-V. (2019). A radical point of view on dissonance theory. In E. Harmon-Jones (Ed.), Cognitive dissonance: Reexamining a pivotal theory in psychology (p. 41–61). American Psychological Association.

Beharrell, B., & Denison, T. J. (1995). Involvement in a routine food shopping context. British Food Journal. Vol. 97, No. 4, pp. 24–29.

Chang, C., & Tseng, A. (2014). The post-purchase communication strategies for supporting on-line impulsive buying. Computers in Human Behavior, Vol. 39, No. 1, pp. 393–403.

Churchilor G. A., & Peter J. (2003). Marketing: creating value for customers. São Paulo: Saraiva.

Connole, R. J., Benson, J. D., & Khera, I. P. (1977). Cognitive dissonance among innovators. Journal of the Academy of Marketing Science. Vol. 5, No. 1–2, pp. 9–20.

Cummings, W. H., & Venkatesan, M. (1976). Cognitive dissonance and consumer behavior: a review of the evidence. Journal of Marketing Research, Vol. 13, No. 3, pp. 303–308.

Deutsch, R., & Strack, F. (2008). Variants of judgment and decision making: The perspective of the reflective-impulsive model. In H. Plessner, C. Betsch, & T. Betsch (Eds.), Intuition in judgment and decision making (p. 39–53). Lawrence Erlbaum Associates Publishers.

Deutsch, R., Gawronski, B., & Hofmann, W. (Eds.). (2016). Reflective and impulsive determinants of human behavior. Psychology Press, Routledge.

Devine, P. G., Hamilton, D. L. E., & Ostrom, T. M. (1994). Social cognition: impact on social psychology. Academic Press.

Elliot, A. J., & Devine, P. G. (1994). On the motivational nature of cognitive dissonance: dissonance as psychological discomfort. Journal of Personality and Social Psychology, Vol. 67, No. 3, pp. 382–394.

Felser, G. (1997). Advertising and consumer psychology: an introduction. Schäffer-Poeschel, Stuttgart.

Festinger, L. (1957). A theory of cognitive dissonance. Stanford University Press.

Festinger, L. (1985). A theory of cognitive dissonance. Stanford University Press, Stanford.

Foxall, G. R. (2002). Consumer behaviour analysis (Vol. 3). Taylor & Francis.

Godin, S. (2018). This is marketing: you can't be seen until you learn to see. Penguin, New York.

Harmon-Jones (2019), Cognitive dissonance: Reexamining a pivotal theory in psychology (p. 141–157). American Psychological Association.

Harmon-Jones, E., & Mills, J. (1999). Cognitive dissonance: progress on a pivotal theory in social psychology. American Psychological Association.

Hawkins, D. I., & Mothersbaugh, D. L. (2010). Consumer behavior: building marketing strategy. Boston: McGraw-Hill Irwin.

Holloway, R. J. (1967). An experiment on consumer dissonance. Journal of Marketing, Vol. 31, No.1, pp. 39–43.

Hoyer, W. D., Macinnis, D. J., & Pieters, R. (2001). Customer behavior. Boston, Houghton Mifflin Company.

Iram, M., & Chacharkar, D. Y. (2017). Model of impulse buying behavior. BVIMSR's Journal of Management Research, Vol. 9, No. 1, pp. 45–53.

Knox, R. E., & Inkster, J. A. (1968). Post-decision dissonance at post time. Journal of Personality and Social Psychology, Vol. 8, No. 4, pp. 319–323.

Koller, M., & Salzberger, T. (2007). Cognitive dissonance as a relevant construct throughout the decision-making and consumption process: an empirical investigation related to a package tour. Journal of Customer Behaviour, Vol. 6, N. 3, pp. 217–227.

Korgaonkar, P. K., & Moschis, G. P. (1982). An experimental study of cognitive dissonance, product involvement, expectations, performance and consumer judgement of product performance. Journal of Advertising, Vol. 11, No. 3, pp. 32–44.

Laird, J. D. (2007). Feelings: The perception of self. Oxford University Press.

Laurent, G., & Kapferer, J. N. (1985). Measuring consumer involvement profiles. Journal of Marketing Research, Vol. 22, No. 1, pp. 41–53.

Losch, M. E., & Cacioppo, J. T. (1990). Cognitive dissonance may enhance sympathetic tonus, but attitudes are changed to reduce negative affect rather than arousal. Journal of Experimental Social Psychology. Vol. 26, No. 4, pp. 289–304.

Mayer, R. E. (2005). Cognitive theory of multimedia learning. In R. E. Mayer (Ed.), The Cambridge Handbook of Multimedia Learning (pp. 31–48). New York: Cambridge University Press.

Mills, J. (2019). Improving the 1957 version of dissonance theory. In E. Harmon-Jones (Ed.), Cognitive dissonance: Reexamining a pivotal theory in psychology (p. 27–39). American Psychological Association.

Mittal, B. (1989). A Theoretical analysis of two recent measures of involvement. Advances in Consumer Research, 16(1).

Mowen, J. C., & Minor, M. (1995). Customer behavior. New Jersey: Prentice Hall Inc.

Nunes, J. C., & Drèze, X. (2006). The endowed progress effect: how artificial advancement increases effort. Journal of Consumer Research, Vol. 32, No. 4, pp. 504–512.

Oliver, R.L. (1997). Satisfaction: a behavioral perspective on the consumer. Boston: McGraw-Hill.

Pepels, W. (2005). Käuferverhalten: Basiswissen für Kaufentscheidungen von Konsumenten und Organisationen; mit Aufgaben und Lösungen. Erich Schmidt.

Pittman, T. S. (1975). Attribution of arousal as mediator in dissonance reduction. Journal of Experimental Social Psychology. Vol. 11, No. 1, pp. 53–63.

Simpson, B., & Willer, R. (2008). Altruism and indirect reciprocity: the interaction of person and situation in prosocial behavior. Social Psychology Quarterly, Vol. 71, No. 1, pp. 37–52.

Sofi, S. A., & Najar, S. A. (2018). Impact of personality influencers on psychological paradigms: an empirical discourse of big five framework and impulsive buying behaviour. European Research on Management and Business Economics, Vol. 24, No. 2, pp. 71–81.

Stone, J., & Cooper, J. (2001). A self-standards model of cognitive dissonance. Journal of Experimental Social Psychology, 37(3), pp. 228–243.

Stone, R., Cooper, S., & Cant, R. (2013). The value of peer learning in undergraduate nursing education: A systematic review. ISRN nursing, 2013.

Sweeney, J., & Chew, M. (2000). Consumer-brand relationships: an exploratory study in the services context. In: Consumer-brand relationships: an exploratory study in the services context (pp. 1234–1238). Promaco Conventions Pty. Ltd.

Venkatraman, V., & Huettel, S. A. (2012). Strategic control in decision-making under uncertainty. European Journal of Neuroscience, Vol. 35, No. 7, pp. 1075–1082.

Wood, M. (2005). Discretionary unplanned buying in consumer society. Journal of Consumer Behavior, Vol. 4, pp. 268–281.

Xiao, S. H., & Nicholson, M. (2013). A multidisciplinary cognitive behavioural framework of impulse buying: a systematic review of the literature. International Journal of Management Reviews, Vol. 15, No. 3, pp. 333–356.

Zaichkowsky, J. L. (1985). Measuring the involvement construct. Journal of Consumer Research, Vol. 12, No. 3, pp. 341–352.

Zanna, M. P., & Cooper, J. (1974). Dissonance and the pill: an attribution approach to studying the arousal properties of dissonance. Journal of Personality and Social Psychology, Vol. 29, No. 5, pp. 703–709.

CHAPTER 4

The Affect State

Abstract The chapter analyzes the role of the affect state on the onset of cognitive dissonance after an impulse buying. More specifically, it has deepened its influence on the way consumers build their decision process, as well as the way it impacts on the consequence of a purchase decisions, depending on whether it is positive or negative.

Keywords Affect state • Decision process • Cognitive dissonance

The term affectivity refers to an aspect of human psychic functions, defining the spectrum of emotions and feelings both positive (e.g., contentment, satisfaction, or serenity) and negative (loneliness, anger, sadness, frustration). When we refer to the concept of a consumer's emotional state toward a product, specifically during the purchasing process, we are concentrating our attention on the emotional aspects deriving from it. Affectivity is a basic concept in marketing studies, notwithstanding underestimated. Often, a consumer tends to attribute the reasons for his behavior to the sphere of rationality; on the contrary, each of his actions has a so-called affective component. The emotional state pre-existing or contemporary to the purchasing process can considerably influence purchasing choices, and it is mainly caused by attitude. It can be defined as the overall psychological orientation, expressed in terms of evaluation

© The Author(s), under exclusive license to Springer Nature
Switzerland AG 2021
G. Mattia et al., *Online Impulse Buying and Cognitive Dissonance*,
https://doi.org/10.1007/978-3-030-65923-3_4

(positive or negative) relative to a concept and characterized by a certain duration. A positive attitude toward a product will increase the likelihood of a certain behavior, affecting both intention and actual purchase (Smith et al. 2008). There are three dimensions forming the attitude: (1) cognitive, (2) affective, and (3) behavioral. Given the same attitude, the mood (i.e., the emotional state of an individual) significantly impacts on customer's decision-making process (Park et al. 2006). On their part, emotions, positive and negative, strongly influence impulse buying (Beatty and Ferrell 1998).

Previous studies have investigated the effect of the incidental state of mind on the reduction of cognitive dissonance. Scholars manipulated the affect state of the involved participants to the experiments after the onset of dissonance and reported coherent findings with a congruent mood effect. In fact, a negative mood coupled with dissonance becomes more negative in individuals who went through a negative experience. On the one hand, the involvement to adjust the negative effect, thus reducing the dissonance, is increased by a negative mood. On the contrary, a positive mood compensates the negative effect of dissonance, resulting in less motivation to neutralize its negative effect. This result depends on the fact that sensitivity to a certain stimulus improves when their value corresponded to the observer's mood (Jones and Kelly 2009; Mayer et al. 1992). In particular, Jonas et al. (2006) observed that post-purchase dissonance coupled with mood affects the urgency to reduce the dissonance itself. A negative mood combined with post-decisional dissonance increases the need to get further information, while the positive one produces its decrease.

With regard to the positive emotional state, it has been repeatedly demonstrated how it can play a central role in the modulation of cognitive control (Goschke and Bolte 2014; Dreisbach and Fischer 2012). A positive emotional state reduces the so-called proactive control, that is, the use of context information (Fröber and Dreisbach 2012, 2014; van Wouwe et al. 2011), thus allowing a greater capacity to respond to unforeseen events. In addition, there is much evidence that positive emotional state induces greater cognitive flexibility (Wang et al. 2017; Dreisbach 2006), while improving creative problem solving (Estrada et al. 1994), reducing response conflicts (Xue et al. 2013), and broadening attention (Rowe et al. 2007). It can therefore be considered that, in the context of the relationship between impulse buying and cognitive dissonance, the positive affect state can play a moderating role in the onset of the latter, thanks to the cognitive flexibility mechanism mentioned above.

To summarize, incidental mood increases the ambition to influence regulation: when experiencing a negative mood, one is driven to reduce the negative effect of dissonance, while a positive one pushes and motivates to maintain their emotional state or cope a negative threat. It has to be noted as well that, according to the sentiment-information hypothesis (Schwarz 1990), the emotional states reveal the relationship between people and their current environment. Negative moods attest that the environment is hostile and, in this context, people strive to minimize negative outcomes, processing the information according to a detail-oriented style, which implies a selective attention. In turn, when people experience a positive mood, they do not rely on this specific kind of behavior, as it helps them feel in a safe and satisfying environment.

One additional consequence is that the value of the emotional state determines the way people approach the style of information processing. The negative mood suggests a systematic processing, while the positive one determines a heuristic processing (Bohner et al. 1995). Systematic processing involves considering all the information meticulously and rationally, and is therefore cognitively expensive (Petty and Cacioppo 1996). On the contrary, heuristic processing is more prone to the use of quick and peripheral thinking styles, allowing a saving of cognitive resources for other tasks. For instance, consumers in a negative mood are a more likely to change their attitude when exposed to strong arguments, while those in a positive mood change their attitude apart from the strength of the arguments (Bless et al. 1990).

Furthermore, when people are aware that their mood can be attributed to an irrelevant cause, the consequent effects terminate to be observed (Sinclair et al. 1994). In a situation of cognitive dissonance, the state of dissonance has shown to have stimulating properties, and because of that the change of attitude involves consciously controlled processing, since consumers have to make a deliberate effort to justify their counter-attitudinal behavior. For example, the change of attitude terminates to be observed if the participant does not focus on dissonant elements (Zanna and Aziza 1976). Pairwise, dissonance affects explicit rather than implicit attitudes (Gawronski and Strack 2004). Explicit attitudes imply cognitively expensive control processes, whereas implicit ones determine less expensive automatic processes.

Since the affective dimension is an essential component of the purchasing process, it allows the creation of stimuli and symbols that can be effective in the consumer influence process. Music, characters, and codes associated with brands constitute communication stimuli that contribute to the improvement of affective evaluations. In fact, emotionality represents a lever which marketers activate to goad the purchasing behavior, including, for example, customer loyalty and impulse buying.

The practitioner who expresses the intention to leverage impulse buying should, therefore, study the emotional state with which a consumer enters a store or purchases on-line. Then, it will be necessary to use the appropriate communication tools to propose an engaging offer which creates a state of empathy between the consumer and the product. The affective dimension must be able to enter more and more into the decision-making process, and product offerings must be considered as an instant solution that the customer perceives during the purchase. When all these conditions happen, the consumer's attitude toward the product will change in a positive way and there will be positive results in terms of impulse buying.

References

Beatty, S. E., & Ferrell, M. E. (1998). Impulse buying: Modeling its precursors. Journal of Retailing, Vol. 74, No. 2, pp. 169–191.

Bless, H., Bohner, G., Schwarz, N., & Strack, F. (1990). Mood and persuasion: A cognitive response analysis. Personality and Social Psychology Bulletin, Vol. 16, No. 2, pp. 331–345.

Bohner, G., Moskowitz, G. B., & Chaiken, S. (1995). The interplay of heuristic and systematic processing of social information. European Review of Social Psychology, Vol. 6, No. 1, pp. 33–68.

Dreisbach, G. (2006). How positive affect modulates cognitive control: the costs and benefits of reduced maintenance capability. Brain and Cognition, Vol. 60, No. 1, pp. 11–19.

Dreisbach, G., & Fischer, R. (2012). Conflicts as aversive signals. Brain and Cognition, 78(2), pp. 94–98.

Estrada, C. A., Isen, A. M., & Young, M. J. (1994). Positive affect improves creative problem solving and influences reported source of practice satisfaction in physicians. Motivation and Emotion, Vol. 18, No. 4, pp. 285–299.

Fröber, K., & Dreisbach, G. (2012). How positive affect modulates proactive control: reduced usage of informative cues under positive affect with low arousal. Frontiers in Psychology, Vol. 3, No. 1, Art. 265, pp. 1–14.

Fröber, K., & Dreisbach, G. (2014). The differential influences of positive affect, random reward, and performance-contingent reward on cognitive control. Cognitive, Affective, & Behavioral Neuroscience, Vol. 14, No. 2, pp. 530–547.

Gawronski, B., & Strack, F. (2004). On the propositional nature of cognitive consistency: Dissonance changes explicit, but not implicit attitudes. Journal of Experimental Social Psychology, Vol. 40, No. 4, pp. 535–542.

Goschke, T., & Bolte, A. (2014). Emotional modulation of control dilemmas: the role of positive affect, reward, and dopamine in cognitive stability and flexibility. Neuropsychologia, Vol. 62, pp. 403–423.

Jonas, E., Graupmann, V., & Frey, D. (2006). The influence of mood on the search for supporting versus conflicting information: dissonance reduction as a means of mood regulation? Personality and Social Psychology Bulletin, Vol. 32, No. 1, pp. 3–15.

Jones, E. E., & Kelly, J. R. (2009). No pain, no gains: negative mood leads to process gains in idea-generation groups. Group Dynamics: Theory, Research, and Practice, Vol. 13, No. 2, pp. 75–88.

Mayer, J. D., Gaschke, Y. N., Braverman, D. L., & Evans, T. W. (1992). Mood-congruent judgment is a general effect. Journal of Personality and Social Psychology, Vol. 63, No. 1, pp. 119–132.

Park, C. W., MacInnis, D. J., & Priester, J. R. (2006). Beyond attitudes: attachment and consumer behavior. Seoul National Journal, Vol. 12, No. 2, pp. 3–36.

Petty, R. E., & Cacioppo, J. T. (1996). Attitudes and persuasion: classic and contemporary approaches. Westview Press.

Rowe, G., Hirsh, J. B., & Anderson, A. K. (2007). Positive affect increases the breadth of attentional selection. Proceedings of the National Academy of Sciences, Vol. 104, No. 1, pp. 383–388.

Schwarz, N. (1990). Feelings as information: informational and motivational functions of affective states. In: Higgins, E.T., Sorrentino, R., (eds): Handbook of motivation and cognition: foundations of social behavior, Vol. 2. Guilford Press, pp. 527–561.

Sinclair, R. C., Mark, M. M., & Clore, G. L. (1994). Mood-related persuasion depends on (mis) attributions. Social Cognition, Vol. 12, No. 4, pp. 309–326.

Smith, J. R., Terry, D. J., Manstead, A. S., Louis, W. R., Kotterman, D., & Wolfs, J. (2008). The attitude–behavior relationship in consumer conduct: The role of norms, past behavior, and self-identity. The Journal of Social Psychology, Vol. 148, No. 3, pp. 311–334.

van Wouwe, N. C., Band, G. P., & Ridderinkhof, K. R. (2011). Positive affect modulates flexibility and evaluative control. Journal of Cognitive Neuroscience, Vol. 23, No. 3, pp. 524–539.

Wang, Z., Singh, S. N., Li, Y. J., Mishra, S., Ambrose, M., & Biernat, M. (2017). Effects of employees' positive affective displays on customer loyalty intentions:

an emotions as social information perspective. Academy of Management Journal, Vol. 60, No. 1, pp. 109–129.

Xue, S., Cui, J., Wang, K., Zhang, S., Qiu, J., & Luo, Y. (2013). Positive emotion modulates cognitive control: an event-related potentials study. Scandinavian Journal of Psychology, Vol. 54, No. 2, pp. 82–88.

Zanna, M. P., & Aziza, C. (1976). On the interaction of repression-sensitization and attention in resolving cognitive dissonance. Journal of Personality, Vol. 44, No. 4, pp. 577–593.

CHAPTER 5

Measuring the Constructs of Impulse Buying, Cognitive Dissonance, and Affect State

Abstract The chapter presents the scales which will be adopted in the empirical study (Chap. 10) to measure the constructs of impulse buying, cognitive dissonance, and affect state. In particular, the impulse buying tendency scale, the Sweeney scale, and the PANAS scale will be used. The functioning of each scale is described, alongside their experimental validation.

Keywords Impulse buying tendency scale • Sweeney scale • PANAS scale • validation

Several scales have been developed in the literature to identify the dimensions that influence the consumer purchasing process. In line with the objectives of the present research, in this paragraph we will examine three different types of scales developed to analyze impulse buying (impulsive buying tendency scale), the cognitive dissonance (Sweeney scale), and the positive and negative affect states (PANAS scale). Subsequently, we examine the elements that contextualize our research, namely on-line impulse purchase drivers, pc-based on-line shopping, and the main characteristics of millennials, which represent the target on which the survey is addressed.

© The Author(s), under exclusive license to Springer Nature
Switzerland AG 2021
G. Mattia et al., *Online Impulse Buying and Cognitive Dissonance*,
https://doi.org/10.1007/978-3-030-65923-3_5

THE IMPULSE BUYING TENDENCY SCALE (IBTS)

The IBTS scale (Verplanken and Herabadi 2001) consists of 20 items measuring the two dimensions of the impulse buying tendency: (1) the cognitive dimension (ten items), which concerns the lack of planning in the purchasing decision (example of items: "usually when I buy something I do it without thinking too much" or "usually I think very well before buying something"); and (2) the emotional dimension (ten items), which concerns feelings of excitement, impulse to buy, and imprudence in buying (example of items: "I feel very excited when I see something I would like to buy" or "I'm not the kind of person who falls in love at first sight of what I see in a store"). The response scale is a five-point Likert (1 = absolutely disagree; 5 = absolutely agree), and the items are structured in such a way that high scores indicate a strong impulse buying tendency.

The IBTS was developed and validated after the authors discovered how impulse buying tendency was linked to individual personality traits, including the Big Five (Costa and McCrae 1986). Both dimensions of the scale (cognitive and affective) are related to the extroversion of the individual. In particular, the cognitive scale is inversely linked to conscientiousness, the personal need for mental structures, and the evaluation. The affective one, instead, is connected to the lack of autonomy and orientation toward action. The development was carried out through a two-part research, based on the hypothesis that personality constitutes a variable permanently explanatory of individual differences. In the first one, a scale for impulse buying tendency was developed, correlated to measures of personal need for mental structures, evaluation, and cognition. In the second, the impulse buying tendency was linked to the Big Five.

The predictive validity of IBTS was tested by correlating it with measurements of typical impulse buying tendency (first study) and recent impulse buying (second study). In both cases, the scale showed good reliability and effective psychometric properties, offering important implications for the understanding of impulse buying, a broader and more general repository in which personality traits and the behavioral styles of the individual are inserted, both useful for a classification and prediction activity.

As stated before, the impulse buyer uses the purchase of certain products (or categories of products) to express himself or with the aim to belong to a group (Dittmar et al. 1995), and Verplanken and Herabadi research (2001) confirms that impulse buying, residing in the personality

The Sweeney Scale

Although the concept of cognitive dissonance has always been widely discussed in the literature on consumer behavior, a reliable scale of measurement of the phenomenon was not published until 2000. This was the case with the publication of Sweeney (2000), which described the development of a 22-item scale to estimate post-purchase cognitive dissonance. The author suggested that the phenomenon of dissonance included both a cognitive and a purely emotional dimension. The author at first generated a set of 100 items related to cognitive dissonance, derived from four exploratory studies conducted through focus groups. The items were evaluated by 12 consumer behavior experts, who were given the definitions of cognitive and emotional dissonance used in the study. Thus, 72 items (36 cognitive and 36 emotional) were selected. From the 72 items obtained from the exploratory phase, two quantitative phases for the scale refinement were developed. The first was aimed at reducing the initial set, using two samples of students, for a total of 645 individuals, coming from four Australian universities, who were asked to answer a questionnaire, in which they were pushed to think about an important purchase decision, involving a problematic choice between two or more comparable alternatives. From this first phase, 28 of the 72 starting items were maintained. The second phase was aimed at evaluating the robustness of the 28-item scale derived from the previous phase. Two samples were used, belonging to customers of two different types of businesses: a furniture shop and a car radio dealer. Customers were invited to participate in the questionnaire immediately after the purchase was completed. From this second phase, the items were reduced to 22, divided into three dimensions of dissonance: one emotional and two cognitive. The emotional dimension was defined as "the psychological discomfort of the person following the purchase decision". The two cognitive dimensions are (1) the wisdom of purchase and (2) concern over deal. The first consisted of the "awareness on the part of the individual, after the purchase has been made, that the product may not serve him or may not be the most appropriate". The second is illustrated as the "awareness on the part of the individual, after the purchase has been made, that he may have been influenced, against his real will, by salespeople".

34   G. MATTIA ET AL.

Sweeney concluded his study by suggesting that the intensity and the effects of dissonance needed to be studied through all stages of the decision-making process, including the time of repetition of the purchase.

THE PANAS SCALE

The measurement of emotional state has to be considered a fundamental part of emotional research (Mauss and Robinson 2009; Diener et al. 1999). According to several authors (Watson et al. 1988; Watson and Clark 1984; Tellegen 1982), affective state can be divided into two broad and independent factors, namely the positive affect state (PA) and the negative affect state (NA). While the positive affect state reflects favorable involvement with the environment, the negative affect state is a general element of emotional distress, there including feelings and emotions such as being nervous, miserable, or upset. Aimed at facilitating a precise definition of these factors, Watson et al. (1988) developed a set of items for measuring positive and negative affect states (PANAS), which consists of two scales of ten elements (one for positive and one for negative). PANAS has proven to be valid among different samples, time intervals, and languages (e.g., Rush and Hofer 2014; Merz et al. 2013; Crawford and Henry 2004).

The PANAS is based on a self-reported questionnaire. Both positive and negative affect states are related to emotions expressed through a list of adjectives, whose presence is evaluated through a five-point Likert scale (1 = not at all or slightly; 5 = extremely). With reference to the two subscales, a high level of positive affect state is referred to a person full of energy, concentration, and vitality; a high level of negative affect state corresponds instead to a person in a state of affliction.

The development phase of the scale was based on a list of 60 terms from the Zevon and Tellegen (1982) analysis, which are considered as indicators relatively precise. Through several purification cycles, researchers arrived to retain ten terms for adjectives pertaining to the two subscales:

- Positive affect state: attentive, active, alert, excited, enthusiastic, determined, inspired, proud, interested, strong.
- Negative affect: afraid, ashamed, distressed, guilty, hostile, irritable, jittery, nervous, scared upset.

The PANAS scale was tested on three different types of samples: a non-clinical student sample, a non-clinical adult sample, and a hospital sample, obtaining a Cronbach alpha greater than 0.85 for both constructs in all the three samples. The brevity and ease of understanding and rating make the scale a reliable tool for measuring affective state that has been positively adopted over the years.

References

Costa, P. T. Jr., & McCrae, R. R. (1986). Major contributions to personality psychology. In Modgil, S., and Modgil, C. (eds), Hans Eysenck: Consensus and Controversy. Barcombe Lewes: Falmer, pp. 63–72, 86, 87.

Crawford, J. R., & Henry, J. (2004). The Positive and Negative Affect Schedule (PANAS): Construct validity, measurement properties and normative data in a large non-clinical sample. British Journal of Clinical Psychology, 43, pp. 245–265.

Rush, J., & Hofer, S. M. (2014). Differences in Within- and Between-Person Factor Structure of Positive and Negative Affect: Analysis of Two Intensive Measurement Studies Using Multilevel Structural Equation Modeling. Psychological Assessment, 26(2).

Diener, E., Suh, E. M., Lucas, R. E., & Smith, H. L. (1999). Subjective well-being: three decades of progress. Psychological Bulletin, Vol. 125, No. 2, pp. 276.

Dittmar, H., Beattie, J., & Friese, S. (1995). Gender identity and material symbols: Objects and decision considerations in impulse purchases. Journal of Economic Psychology, Vol. 16, No. 3, pp. 491–511.

Mauss, I. B., & Robinson, M. D. (2009). Measures of emotion: a review. Cognition and Emotion, Vol. 23, No. 2, pp. 209–237.

Merz, E. L., Malcarne, V. L., Roesch, S. C., Ko, C. M., Emerson, M., Roma, V. G., & Sadler, G. R. (2013). Psychometric properties of Positive and Negative Affect Schedule (PANAS) original and short forms in an African American community sample. Journal of Affective Disorders, Vol. 151, No. 3, pp. 942–949.

Sweeney, J. C. (2000). Cognitive dissonance after purchase: a multidimensional scale. Psychology & Marketing, Vol.17, No. 5, pp. 369–385.

Tellegen, A. (1982). Brief manual for the multidimensional personality questionnaire. Unpublished manuscript, University of Minnesota, Minneapolis, pp. 1031–1010.

Verplanken, B., & Herabadi, A. (2001). Individual differences in impulse buying tendency: feeling and no thinking. European Journal of Personality, Vol. 15(S1), pp. S71–S83.

Watson, D., & Clark, L. A. (1984). Negative affectivity: the disposition to experience aversive emotional states. Psychological Bulletin, Vol. 96, No. 3, pp. 465.

Watson, D., Clark, L. A., & Tellegen, A. (1988). Development and validation of brief measures of positive and negative affect: the PANAS scales. Journal of Personality and Social Psychology, Vol. 54, No. 6, pp. 1063–1070.

Zevon, M. A., & Tellegen, A. (1982). The structure of mood change: An idiographic/nomothetic analysis. Journal of Personality and Social Psychology, Vol. 43, No. 1, pp. 111–122.

CHAPTER 6

On-line Consumer Behavior and Technology Acceptance Models

Abstract This chapter intends to offer a review of technology acceptance and behavioral models, with the purpose to better comprehend the enabling and disabling factors which encourage consumers to adopt (or refuse) e-commerce digital platforms for their purchases.

Keywords Technology acceptance • e-commerce • Digital platforms

The on-line sales market is rapidly expanding. According to Google's consumer barometer (2015) and Eurostat (2017), about two-thirds of the European population make purchases on-line. In 2019 (Casaleggio 2020), data show that the number of users accessing the internet is around 4.7 billion (60% of the total population), more than half of whom reside in the Asia-Pacific region. Last year, 80% of internet users searched on-line for a product or service, and 74% made at least one purchase, for a total of about three billion shoppers. The B2C on-line commerce business is estimated in 2019 at about 3.5 billion dollars, 20% more than the previous year, and it is expected that in 2020 it could exceed five billion dollars.

At the European level, 85% of the population accesses the internet, with Europe at the top of the world ranking by penetration index. In Europe, on-line sales reach 309 billion euros (10% more than 2018), with

© The Author(s), under exclusive license to Springer Nature
Switzerland AG 2021
G. Mattia et al., *Online Impulse Buying and Cognitive Dissonance*,
https://doi.org/10.1007/978-3-030-65923-3_6

electronic products at 76 billion euros. More than 64% of shoppers use a mobile device, while the remaining part a personal computer.

After a transitional period in which the user experience and the learning curve required consolidation, and after technological and infrastructure improvements (i.e. transaction security and higher connection speed), the increased consumer confidence and competence made on-line purchases accessible and efficient. More and more consumers are perceiving the digital market as an attractive and enjoyable opportunity, contributing to increase their buying intentions (Chiang and Dholakia 2003).

Not only the consumer experience has changed with the growth and emergence of the e-commerce market, but this commercial development has profoundly changed the industry. The on-line channel has now become a natural component of the supply system, just as the physical one. Today, in fact, e-commerce is flexible and interactive, with an infinite potential for communication between individuals and companies (van der Heijden et al. 2003).

The on-line market allows completely new methods for distribution, communication, and transaction compared to traditional retail channels. Looking at the contemporary on-line market, the consumer is now in a position to use technology to search, find, and buy any good or service, so much that many platforms also provide incentives for continuous purchases (the so-called continuous shopping), such as saved shopping carts, wish lists, rewards, and discounts (Kim and Kim 2004). Some researchers suggest that the use of virtual shopping has a strong power to influence a consumer to repeat the action habitually, creating a sort of dependence from the tool (Soto-Acosta et al. 2014).

On the offering side, Weideli (2013) described the changes experienced by sellers, whose supply chains now consist of a central warehouse which can be located anywhere, being only necessary to create inventories and distribute goods. Furthermore, Wong (2018) discussed five of the year's most important trends, including the role of social media on the growth of e-commerce. Social media have become an essential engine for the success of digital commerce, deeply influencing purchasing decisions. Overall, the increased competition in the market has also increased advertising costs, prompting e-commerce brands to invest in new brainstorming creative approaches to reach consumers.

We can consider two distinct ways through which consumers decide, or refuse, to buy through e-commerce. The first is the channel's ability to meet the demand-related needs (availability, quality, price, etc.), the completeness, and reliability of the information, up to the ability to reassure data protection. A second has more to do with the positive attitude and the willingness that consumers show using a certain available technology.

In general, acceptance is defined as an antagonism of the term rejection and refers to the positive decision to make use of an innovation. User acceptance and trust are key components for the development of any new technology (Simon et al. 2001), and technology acceptance models and theories have been applied to understand and predict user behavior. Some studies have used traditional models to conduct research on the subject, while others have combined previous models by creating new constructs (Taherdoost 2018). More than one theoretical approach is needed to fully understand the consumer acceptance of technology.

The model of the theory of reasoned action (TRA) (Fishbein and Ajzen 1975) is the basis for investigating the behavior of individuals about the use of technology. In this model, human behavior is explained through three main cognitive components: attitudes, social norms, and intentions (Lai 2017). The main purpose of TRA is to understand individuals' voluntary behavior by examining the basic motivation that drives them to perform an action. According to the theory, the intention to carry out a behavior precedes the actual one. Reasoned action theory suggests that stronger intentions imply a greater likelihood to behave, and hence the behavioral intention stems from the belief that the execution of the behavior will lead to a subsequent result.

The theory requires that the behavior be clearly defined according to four concepts: action, target, context, and time. The scope of TRA is broad, but the theory presented some limitations and required constant refinement and revision. Ajzen acknowledged that some behaviors are more likely to imply control issues than others. Seen from this point of view, it became clear that every intention is an objective whose achievement is subject to a certain degree of uncertainty. Because the TRA focuses on behaviors that people engage in, the theory is limited to the ability to predict behaviors that require opportunity, capacity, conditions, and/or resources.

The evolution of the TRA is defined as the theory of planned behavior (TPB) (Ajzen 1991), conceived to improve the predictive power of the TRA model. In fact, according to the TPB, attitude toward behavior, subjective norms, and perceived behavioral control are the factors that shape an individual's intentions and drive them to perform a certain behavior. In order to improve the predictive power of the TPB model in the field of technology, Davis (1986) gave birth to the technology acceptance model (TAM), introducing variables such as the perceived availability of a certain technological service and the level of technological innovation. Three years later, Davis (1989) used TAM to explain the user's behavior about computers. The goal was to explain the general determinants of computer acceptance and offered a way to predict users' behavior compared to a wide range of computer technologies. The TAM model, in its basic form, included and tested two specific beliefs: perceived utility (PU) and perceived ease of use (PEU). In this way, the intention to use is controlled by the individual personality which, together with the perceived utility (PU) and the perceived ease of use (PEU), affects a person's mood with respect to the use of a specific technology. The perceived utility (PU) is characterized by the trust placed by individuals toward the use, but above all by the idea that such a use can improve the performance of certain activities. It is the determining factor that strongly influences users' beliefs and expectations regarding the choice to use a technological innovation. The perceived ease of use, on the other hand, refers to the degree to which potential users expect the technology to be used effortlessly.

As previous models, the TAM is subject to various kind of limitations, not least the impossibility to catch the impact of emotional as well as functional needs (Davis et al. 1989). Consequently, in 2000 Venkatesh and Davis extended the model by calling it TAM2. In TAM2 it is hypothesized that the subjective norms exert a direct effect on the intention, at the level of both perceived utility (PU) and the perceived ease of use (PEU). To make TAM2 better performing in terms of predictive power, Venkatesh and Bala (2008) developed an integrated version named TAM3, which included individual differences, technology characteristics, social influence, and facilitation conditions, that is, the determinants of perceived utility and perceived ease of use.

Besides the models of technology acceptance, it is also necessary to mention those related to the diffusion of technology, which constitute a logical integration of the latter. The study of innovations' spread took off in the field of rural sociology in the United States, in the 1920s and 1930s. However, three decades were necessary before a formalized theory of innovation's diffusion was released. In 1963, Everett Rogers formulated the diffusion of innovation theory (DIT), used at both individual and organizational levels (Dearing and Cox 2018). The DIT model examines a variety of innovations by introducing four key issues (time, communication channels, innovation, social system) that influence the spread of a new idea or of a new product. In addition to these elements, one-fifth is constituted by the so-called adopters, which are the minimum units of analysis (they can be individuals, organizations, clusters within social networks, or countries) (Taherdoost 2018). Three main components are integrated through this model: the characteristics of the adoption, the characteristics of the innovation, and the decision-making toward the innovation. The characteristics of an innovation are related to the evaluation by potential users. An innovation is primarily assessed against the relative advantage, namely its perceived efficiency compared to the current procedures. Second, the assessment is based on compatibility with the existing system, complexity or learning difficulties, traceability, reinvention of potential, and observed effects. These qualities interact and are judged and considered as a whole. Adoption characteristics were sought at first in individual personality traits, then in skills and motivations. The latter vary depending on the situation and, unlike personality traits, have a great impact on the likelihood of a potential user to adopt an innovation. In fact, potential users possessing a strong motivation are capable to make the necessary changes for adoption, and the symbolic meaning of an innovation can influence motivation by encouraging or discouraging its adoption.

Finally, the decision-making process was divided by Rogers into five phases: awareness, interest, evaluation, experimenting, and adoption. In later variants of the innovation diffusion model, Rogers modified the terminology of the five phases: knowledge, persuasion, decision, implementing, and confirmation. The change in terminology occurred due to some criticism regarding the possibility of rejection by an individual, both during and after the adoption process. Thus, the adoption of a new idea, or product, or even a habit (i.e., "an innovation") does not take place simultaneously within a social system; rather, it is a process by which some people are more likely to adopt innovation than others. More specifically, those who immediately adopt an innovation possess different characteristics than people adopting it at a later stage. In fact, when innovation is promoted within a target population, it is important to understand the characteristics of that population, since it is precisely these framework that will prove to be an aid or obstacle to the adoption of an innovation. In this respect, there are five categories of users corresponding to as many attitudes and behaviors as innovation's adopters. Innovators are people who want to be the first to try an innovation. They are adventurous, with a strong propensity to take risks and often are those promoting on their own the development of new ideas. Pioneers can be defined as opinion leaders. They enjoy leadership roles and positively embrace opportunities for change. In addition, they are aware of the need to change and are therefore comfortable with the adoption of new ideas. The early majority, on the other hand, are those who are rarely leaders, but still more likely to adopt new ideas than the average of people. They generally need evidence about how innovation works before they are willing to adopt it. Skepticism about change characterizes people pertaining to the category of the late majority. They are only willing to adopt an innovation after it has been tested by the early majority. In the end, the last category is that of the laggards. These people are traditional and very conservative; they possess a strong resistance to modify their habits and are therefore the most difficult group to engage.

According to Rogers, the diffusion of innovations is explained by a graph whose horizontal axis is the categorization of consumer groups adopting a new technology, while the vertical axis represents the market share of innovation. Like any innovation, the market share curve, which assumes a normal distribution, will reach saturation level at the peak of its spread.

Aimed at reaching an integrated framework, Venkatesh et al. (2003) compared eight dominant theories and models on the acceptance of technology applicable to the human sciences domain. The new theory, called unified theory of acceptance use of technology (UTAUT), represents an attempt to integrate the TAM with other decision-making theories such as the theory of reasoned action (TRA), the theory of planned behavior (TPB), the social cognitive theory (SCT) (Bandura 1977), and the innovation diffusion theory (IDT). The UTAUT model refers to the perceived utility as to a performance expectation and the perceived ease compared to the required effort. This theory is characterized by the adoption of two additional key constructs: the social influences, referring to the regulation of the self-image, and the facilitating conditions, defined as the extent to which an individual believes that an organizational and a technical infrastructure able to support the use of the new technology be in place.

In 2012, Venkatesh et al. incorporated three new constructs in the UTAUT model: the hedonic motivation, price, and habit. This new model has been called the unified theory of the acceptance and use of technology 2 (UTAUT2).

Narrowing the field to e-shopping, the most important drivers inducing consumers to adopt a new technology are represented by the ease of use and perceived utility (Gefen and Straub 2000). The ease to place an order, transaction security, privacy protection, certainty of delivery times, and return management are all facilitators to make use of an e-retailer. As is evident, in this set of elements aspects related to the digitization of purchases, as well as those of a physical nature, for example logistics, simultaneously interact. Therefore, e-retailer requires a composite and often complex organization, which must be maintained in full effectiveness and efficiency to ensure adequate levels of service. On the other hand, it is equally important that the web interface be designed with great accuracy, to ensure a high-level experience, which convinces the consumer to complete an act of purchase. In other words, it is not possible to rely only on price convenience, because this aspect, taken on its own, is insufficient. Rather, there is a theme of a more general convenience and appeal. Especially when thinking about repeated purchases, the fulfillment of which mainly depends on a complex set of expectations and perceptions, the e-commerce platform is called to steadily comply with performance requirements, such as technical and functional quality, alongside the product competitiveness. Of course, the sensitivity, or rather the weight that is attributed by the individuals to the aspects just mentioned, changes according to the type of users. For example, those with a strong familiarity with technology are likely to take for granted things like transaction security and sensitive data protection. Similarly, this familiarity affects the propensity to shop on-line, rather than in less technologically advanced targets (McCloskey 2004).

Another crucial aspect is customer support, which affects the propensity to become loyal, especially in the case of problems related to the post-purchase either of products or of services (e.g. delays in delivery, defectiveness, poor timeliness of communications). This is a "moment of truth" that fixes in the memory of customers, and influences the propensity to repeated purchases thanks to the delight of a valuable service (Verton 2001).

More generally, the on-line shopping experience contemplates cognitive and emotional aspects and is therefore formed in a complex sphere, for which the understanding of technology acceptance models must integrate with those of consumer psychology (Koufaris 2002). In this sense, transaction costs (i.e., on-line information search) can also guide consumer behavior in the decision to buy or not: more specifically, accessibility, timeliness, and reliability of information have an impact on choices

(Bakos 1997), being able to reduce cognitive efforts and reassure consumers. What stated above has to be reinforced bearing in mind that on-line consumers cannot use all five senses to perform their decisions. Therefore, the quality of the information, the appropriate and detailed representation of the products, as well as the appeal and ability to engage in on-line environment impact on the opinions that they tend to form (Novak et al. 1998, 2000)—the same as happens during a physical shopping experience—and must always be kept high, to gain favorable reactions (Li et al. 1999). This is even more true when thinking about unplanned purchases, as on the web the space-time dimension loses importance compared to physical shopping, increasing the possibility of impulse action (Beatty and Ferrell 1998). If the involvement with the product is high, then we can expect a more positive shopping experience because of the greater interest the consumer possesses toward the purchase (Koufaris 2002). Ultimately, motivations play a significant role in the decision of fulfilling an on-line transaction and serve as important predictors of the purchase decision (van der Heijden 2004).

References

Ajzen, I., 1991. The theory of planned behavior. Organizational Behavior and Human Decision Processes, Vol. 50, No. 2, pp. 179–211.

Bakos, Y. (1997). Reducing buyer search costs: implications for electronic marketplaces. Management Science, Vol. 43, No. 12, pp. 1676–1692.

Bandura, A. (1977), Social Learning Theory, Prentice Hall, Englewood Cliffs, New Jersey.

Beatty, S. E., & Ferrell, M. E. (1998). Impulse buying: Modeling its precursors. Journal of Retailing, Vol. 74, No. 2, pp. 169–191.

Casaleggio e Associati (2020). E-commerce in Italia, 2020. https://www.casaleggio.it/e-commerce/. [Last accessed: June 16, 2020].

Chiang, K., & Dholakia, R. R. (2003). Factors driving consumer intention to shop on-line: an empirical investigation. Journal of Consumer Psychology, Vol. 13, No. 1, pp. 177–183.

Davis, F. (1986). Technology Acceptance Model for empirically testing new end-user information systems: theory and results. PhD thesis MIT Sloan School of Management, Cambridge.

Davis, F., Bagozzi, R., & Warshaw, P. (1989). User acceptance of computer technology: a comparison of two theoretical models. Management Science, Vol. 35, No. 8, pp. 982–1003.

Dearing, J. W., & Cox, J. G. (2018). Diffusion of innovations theory, principles, and practice. Health Affairs, Vol. 37, No. 2, pp. 183–190.

Eurostat (2017). Internet purchases by individuals 2008 to 2017 [statistics]. Available from https://ec.europa.eu/eurostat/data/database [Last accessed: March 6, 2020].

Fishbein, M., & Ajzen, I. (1975). Belief, attitude, intention, and behavior: an introduction to theory and research. Addison-Wesley, Reading, MA.

Gefen, D., & Straub, D. (2000). The relative use of perceived ease of use in IS adoption: a study of e-commerce adoption. Journal of the Association for Information Systems, Vol. 1, No. 8, pp. 1–28.

Google Consumer Barometer (2015). The smart shopper: research and purchase behavior (ROPO). Available at https://www.thinkwithgoogle.com/_qs/documents/3520/CB_Country_Report_15_-_France_1.pdf [Last accessed: 7, July 2020].

Kim, E. Y., & Kim, Y. (2004). Predicting on-line purchase intentions for clothing products. European Journal of Marketing, Vol. 38, No. 7, pp. 883–897.

Koufaris, M. (2002). Applying the technology acceptance model and flow theory to on-line consumer behavior. Information Systems Research. Vol. 13, No. 2, pp. 205–223.

Lai, P. (2017). The literature review of technology adoption models and theories for the novelty technology. Journal of Information Systems and Technology Management, Vol. 14, No. 1, Jan/Apr., 2017 pp. 21–38.

Li, H., Kuo, C., & Rusell, M. G. (1999). The impact of perceived channel utilities, shopping orientations, and demographics on the consumer's on-line buying behavior. Journal of Computer-Mediated Communication, Vol. 5, No. 2, JCMC521.

McCloskey, D., 2004. Evaluating electronic commerce acceptance with the technology acceptance model. Journal of Computer Information Systems, Vol. 44, No. 2, pp. 49–57.

Novak, T. P., Hoffman, D. L., & Yung, Y. F. (1998). Modeling the Structure of the Flow Experience. Informs Marketing Science and the Internet Mini-Conference.

Novak, T. P., Hoffman, D. L., & Yung, Y. (2000). Measuring the customer experience in on-line environments: a structural modeling approach. Marketing science, Vol. 19, No. 1, pp. 22–42.

Simon, B., Bildungssektor, W., Akzeptanzuntersuchung an Hochschulen, E. (2001). Knowledge media in the education system: acceptance research in universities. In W. V. Business. Vienna, Austria.

Soto-Acosta, P., Molina-Castillo, F. J., Lopez-Nicolas, C., & Colomo-Palacios, R. (2014). The effect of information overload and disorganisation on intention to purchase on-line: the role of perceived risk and internet experience. On-line Information Review, Vol. 38 No. 4, pp. 543–561.

Taherdoost, H. (2018). A review of technology acceptance and adoption models and theories. Procedia Manufacturing, 22, 961.

van der Heijden, H. (2004). User acceptance of hedonic information systems. MIS Quarterly (28:4), pp. 695–704.

van der Heijden, H., Verhagen, T., & Creemers, M. (2003). Understanding on-line purchase intentions: contributions from technology and trust perspectives. European Journal of Information Systems, Vol. 12, pp. 41–48.

Venkatesh, V., & Bala, H. (2008). Technology acceptance model 3 and a research agenda on interventions. Decision Sciences, Vol. 39, No. 2, pp. 273–315.

Venkatesh, V., Morris, M. G., Davis G. B., & Davi, F. D. (2003). User acceptance of information technology: towards a unified view. MIS Quarterly, pp. 425–478.

Verton, D. (2001). Not so happy holiday on-line. Computerworld, Vol. 35, No. 1, pp. 1–15.

Weideli, D. (2013). Environmental analysis of US on-line shopping. Journal of Consumer Research, Vol.12, pp. 29–43.

Wong, K. (2018). Top 5 trends driving e-commerce: influential takeaways from the report retailers cannot ignore. Journal of Consumer Research, Vol. 72, No. 1, pp.13–42.

CHAPTER 7

Drivers for On-line Impulse Purchases of Highly Symbolic Products

Abstract The chapter concentrates the attention on the connection between on-line sales channels and impulse purchase. The websites' capacity to engage consumers emotions and trust is analyzed, together with the role of social media, which acting as a peer-to-peer relationships shortens and speeds up the decision process. The result envisages that on-line shopping somehow encourages to impulsivity, especially as far as highly symbolic products are concerned.

Keywords On-line impulse purchases • Highly symbolic products

With the spread of e-commerce, the need to study impulse buying on various web platforms has become of paramount importance, due to the growing impact of this medium as a sales channel. At first sight, it can be argued that digital purchasing behavior has a strong rational dimension, as consumers tend to gather the necessary information and compare different alternatives before making the final decision. However, it is not always possible to make rational choices, and impulse buying has also gained a large role within this new market. Rose et al. (2011), for example, noted that the possibilities for controlling on-line purchases are relatively small. Noteworthy is the establishment of the so-called social commerce, a branch of e-commerce incorporating the use of social media in all types of

© The Author(s), under exclusive license to Springer Nature
Switzerland AG 2021
G. Mattia et al., *Online Impulse Buying and Cognitive Dissonance*,
https://doi.org/10.1007/978-3-030-65923-3_7

47

business activities. Social network users share a huge number of experiences, ranging from mere entertainment to evaluating products and services and leading to influencing others by posting images of their purchases and offer recommendations. The recommendation has not to be considered a fragment of information treated by the consumer as part of his/her product research within the framework of a planned decision, but is a stimulus, triggering the desire to buy without further reasoning (Xiang et al. 2016). Kim and Eastin (2011) recalled how the rapid evolution of on-line shopping produced a real alteration in purchasing behavior, downstream of which one can expect a psychological change in consumers, not least the relationship with cognitive dissonance. George and Yaoyuneyong (2010) argued that on-line shopping is a tool capable of immerging consumers in a participatory shopping experience and reducing cognitive dissonance by resolving uncertainty. Indeed, considering that one of the advantages of on-line shopping is the abundance of information, the phenomenon of cognitive dissonance should be kept under control. Under this respect, Kwon and Lennon (2009) noted instead how the latter can emerge anyway when the information presented is not considered reliable. In fact, the information represents a partial element of evaluation, since there are no methods to test the product physically before the purchase, unlike digital word of mouth, which essentially consists of positive reviews about a product and is able to significantly increase the level of confidence. According to Kim and Eastin (2011), another important concept that affects cognitive dissonance among digital consumers is their motivation, considered as a critical factor to understand their consumption habits within this new environment.

Given the above premises, it is appropriate to make an analytical review of the factors influencing on-line impulse buying of highly symbolic products. First of all, as already mentioned, impulse buying follows a tendency to the impulsiveness of the individual, which depends on the degree of emotional attachment to the product (Bratko et al. 2013), the immediacy of the decision (Amos et al. 2014), and the lack of control over the remorse resulting from the decision (Floh and Madlberger 2013). Impulsive individuals tend to be momentarily pleasure oriented and are unable to rationalize the consequences of their choices (Costa and Laran 2003; Amos et al. 2014). The propensity to materialism is also an antecedent: consumers with these traits are in fact predisposed to buy so that they can express their state to peers (Santini et al. 2019; Banerjee and Dittmar 2008). Materialistic consumers are, therefore, more inclined than others to buy products with a high symbolic value (cars, clothing, technological products) and to exhibit their well-being (Ward and Wackman 1972).

As stated in the previous chapters, the most important and identifying emotional dimension in impulse buying is "the sudden and imperative desire to purchase" (Rook and Hoch 1985); therefore another variable related to the consumer can be traced back to the moods (positive or negative) that manifest themselves at the moment of impulse buying. A negative state of mind leads consumers to buy on impulse to "fight the blues" (Piron 1993), that is, to reduce stress or decrease the negative effect of anxiety (Youn and Faber 2000). On the other hand, positive moods such as joy, pleasure, and enthusiasm are also associated with impulse buying (Beatty and Ferrell 1998), as they fulfill the desire for fun, excitement, and novelty searched by consumers (Piron 1991; Hausman 2000).

Pairwise, not only it can be assumed that impulse buying is pushed by the willingness to achieve the above goals (Podoshen and Andrzejewski 2012), but purchasing pleasure should also be considered, which can change the mood from negative to positive, being able to provide the satisfaction of a need and relaxation from a stressful situation (Yu and Bastin 2010). The hedonistic content, referring to a multi-sensory effect that produces a positive excitement, is capable by itself to induce satisfaction, which in turn is memorized and stimulates subsequent repetitions, in an attempt to obtain a regulation of emotions (Tifferet and Herstein 2012).

With regard to the situational factors, the relationship between the purchasing environment and the consumer's emotions must be taken into account. Situational factors are the result of a combination of environmental and personal traits, playing an important role in specific consumer experiences (Dholakia et al. 2000). Impulse buying is promoted by characteristics inherent to the marketplace and by the atmosphere of a store or a website. The way products are displayed and proposed, the colors used, or the type of information are all variables that influence impulse buying (Peck and Childers 2006), since this kind of stimuli increases people's awareness and trust. An enjoyable context tends in fact to generate positive emotions and increase the perception of a product's value (Davis and Sajtos 2009; Mallalieu and Palan 2006).

Equally, it is also necessary to mention the time and the pleasantness effects of spending time in a shopping environment. Several studies (i.e., Heilman et al. 2002; Donovan et al. 1994) discovered in fact that the increase in time spent doing shopping in an environment perceived as pleasant increases the probability of an impulse purchase. This is due to the prolonged stay, which exposes consumers to unplanned products and to the favorable atmosphere and predisposes them to the purchase intention.

Impulse purchasing decisions also vary according to product categories, frequency of purchase, degree of attraction to a certain product, and price level. According to Bellenger et al. (1978), for example, in certain categories such as jewelry, bakery, and footwear, impulse buying is prevalent, but the frequency of purchases can also lead to impulse choices. In this case, the low frequency of purchase determines more impulsivity, even if the price continues to be a driver of influence, especially during promotions, because it encourages the perception of convenience (Kollat and Willett 1967).

Although there are similarities between physical and on-line shops—both aim to communicate the value of a product and sell it—an on-line transaction is characterized by peculiar elements. Among these it is enough to mention the absence of physicality and the impossibility to try the products, the lack of direct interaction with the sales force, and the total self-management of the purchasing process. The current social and economic changes, the speed, and the number of alternatives offered by internet shopping have considerably increased the possibility to make impulse purchases on-line (de Kervenoael et al. 2009; Sun and Wu 2011). From the perspective of impulse buying on-line, the ability of the website to create consumer awareness of the product on sale, through appropriate presentation and information methods, is therefore crucial. In order to induce impulse buying, in fact, the consumer must be exposed to a product that he or she was not looking for, that is, that he or she was not planning to buy.

In on-line shopping, e-stores and e-commerce platforms can take advantage of all these aspects, since if consumers can navigate alone with self-orientation, the lengthening of navigation can encourage the propensity to purchase impulsively (Iyer 1989), based on the number and intensity of the received stimuli (Rook and Fisher 1995). In fact, the possibility of finding information and comparing products over the entire 24-hour period is an amplifying mechanism of exposure to products, which can be more easily translated into impulse purchasing (Phau and Lo 2004).

It is also worth underlying the effect of on-line payment methods as a possible antecedent for impulse buying. Park and Forney (2004) studied the relationship between credit card use and impulse purchase and found it was positive. More specifically, credit or debit cards can lead to impulse buying because of the speed they allow in concluding a transaction.

Furthermore, many virtual marketplaces offer the possibility of fast payments (the so-called one-click payments). In other words, there is no need to enter the debit or credit card data each time when purchasing, thus reducing the possibility of rethinking.

The impulse purchase can finally depend on the cross-selling and up-selling strategies of a site or e-commerce platform. In the first case, consumer is offered a higher-end product among those he or she is looking for, while in the second case, a consumer looking for a certain product is stimulated to buy complementary products that complete the original purchase, for example, using the formula of "if you bought this one you might need this one" (Levy and Weitz 2007). The above approach can be coupled with promotional initiatives, which help to generate impulse purchases on-line, for example, through the use of flash sales time-bound to make a quick choice so the consumer doesn't miss it out, free shipping (Malester 2006), and promotional codes valid for a limited duration.

In conclusion, it can be said that impulse buying is more likely to occur in the case of products with a high hedonistic content rather than the more trivial and recurring purchases and that occurs more on-line than in physical stores (Amos et al. 2014). Of course, the on-line environment in which the potential transaction will take place should give the consumer a feeling of confidence regarding both the security of the transaction itself, that is, the absence of risk of loss, and the situation, that is, a comfortable and suitable environment for a purchase (McKnight et al. 2002).

References

Amos, C., Holmes, G. R., & Keneson, W. C. (2014). A meta-analysis of consumer impulse buying. Journal of Retailing and Consumer Services, Vol. 21, No. 2, pp. 86–97.

Banerjee, R., & Dittmar, H. (2008). Individual differences in children's materialism: The role of peer relations. Personality and Social Psychology Bulletin, Vol. 34, No. 1, pp. 17–31.

Beatty, S. E., & Ferrell, M. E. (1998). Impulse buying: Modeling its precursors. Journal of Retailing, Vol. 74, No. 2, pp. 169–191.

Bellenger, D. N., Robertson, D. H., & Hirschman, E. C. (1978). Impulse buying varies by product. Journal of Advertising Research, Vol. 18, No. 6, pp. 15–18.

Bratko, D., Butkovic, A., & Bosnjak, M. (2013). Twin study of impulsive buying and its overlap with personality. Journal of Individual Differences, Vol. 34, pp. 8–1.

52 G. MATTIA ET AL.

Costa, F., & Laran, J. (2003). Impulse buying on the internet: antecedents and consequences. In: SMA retail symposium, November.

Davis, R., & Sajtos, L. (2009). Anytime, anywhere: measuring the ubiquitous consumer's impulse purchase behavior. International Journal of Mobile Marketing, Vol. 4, No. 1, pp. 15–22.

de Kervenoael, R., Aykac, D. S. O., & Palmer, M. (2009). On-line social capital: understanding e-impulse buying in practice. Journal of Retailing and Consumer Services, Vol. 16, No. 4, pp. 320–328.

Dholakia, R. R., Zhao, M., Dholakia, N., & Fortin, D. R. (2000). Interactivity and revisits to websites: a theoretical framework. Working Paper, RITIM.

Donovan, R. J., Rossiter, J. R., Marcoolyn, G., & Nesdale, A. (1994). Store atmosphere and purchasing behavior. Journal of Retailing, Vol. 70, No. 3, pp. 283–294.

Floh, A., & Madlberger, M. (2013). The role of atmospheric cues in on-line impulse-buying behavior. Electronic Commerce Research and Applications, Vol. 12, No. 6, pp. 425–439.

George, B. P., & Yaoyuneyong, G. (2010). Impulse buying and cognitive dissonance: a study conducted among the spring break student shoppers. Young Consumers. Vol. 11, No. 4, pp. 291–306.

Hausman, A. (2000). A multi-method investigation of consumer motivations in impulse buying behavior. Journal of Consumer Marketing, Vol. 17, No. 5, pp. 403–426.

Heilman, C. M., Nakamoto, K., & Rao, A. G. (2002). Pleasant surprises: consumer response to unexpected in-store coupons. Journal of Marketing Research, Vol. 39, No. 2, pp. 242–252.

Iyer, E. S. (1989). Unplanned purchasing: knowledge of shopping environment and Time Pressure. Journal of Retailing, Vol. 65, No. 1, 40–58.

Kim, S., & Eastin, M. S. (2011). Hedonic tendencies and the on-line consumer: an investigation of the on-line shopping process. Journal of Internet Commerce, Vol. 10, No. 1, pp. 68–90.

Kollat, D. T., & Willett, R. P. (1967). Customer impulse purchasing behavior. Journal of Marketing Research, Vol. 4, No. 1, pp. 21–31.

Kwon, W. S., & Lennon, S. J. (2009). Reciprocal effects between multichannel retailers' offline and on-line brand images. Journal of Retailing, Vol. 85, No. 3, pp. 376–390.

Levy, M., & Weitz, B. A. (2007). Retailing mangement. McGraw-Hill, Irwin.

Malester, J. (2006). TWICE: this week in consumer electronics. Consumer Electronics, Vol. 21, No. 10, p. 104.

Mallalieu, L., & Palan, K. M. (2006). How good a shopper am I? Conceptualizing teenage girls' perceived shopping competence. Academy of Marketing Science Review, Vol, 2005, No. 5, Available: http://www.amsreview.org/article/mallalieu05-2006.pdf.

McKnight, D. H., Choudhury, V., & Kacmar, C. (2002). Developing and validating trust measures for e-commerce: An integrative typology. Information Systems Research, Vol. 13, No. 3, pp. 334–359.

Park, E. J., & Forney, J. C. (2004). A comparison of impulse buying behavior and credit card use between Korean and American college students. Journal of the Korean Society of Clothing and Textiles, Vol. 28, No. 12, pp. 1571–1582.

Peck, J., & Childers, T. L. (2006). If I touch it, I have to have it: individual and environmental influences on impulse purchasing. Journal of Business Research, Vol. 59, No. 6, pp. 765–769.

Phau, I., & Lo, C. C. (2004). Profiling fashion innovators. Journal of Fashion Marketing and Management: an International Journal. Vol. 8, No. 4, pp. 399–411.

Piron, F. (1991). Defining impulse purchasing. ACR North American Advances.

Piron, F. (1993). A comparison of emotional reactions experienced by planned, unplanned and impulse purchasers. in NA - Advances in Consumer Research Volume 20, eds. Leigh McAlister and Michael L. Rothschild, Provo, UT: Association for Consumer Research, pp. 341–344.

Podoshen, J. S., & Andrzejewski, S. A. (2012). An examination of the relationships between materialism, conspicuous consumption, impulse buying, and brand loyalty. Journal of Marketing Theory and Practice, Vol. 20, No. 3, pp. 319–334.

Rook, D. W., & Fisher, R. J. (1995). Normative influences on impulsive buying behavior. Journal of Consumer Research, Vol. 22, No. 3, pp. 305–313.

Rook, D. W., & Hoch, S. J. (1985). Consuming impulses. Advances in Consumer Research, Vol. 12, No. 1, pp. 23–27.

Rose, S., Hair, N., & Clark, M. (2011). On-line customer experience: a review of the business-to-consumer on-line purchase context. International Journal of Management Reviews, Vol. 13, No. 1, pp. 24–39.

Santini, F. D. O., Ladeira, W. J., Vieira, V. A., Araujo, C. F., & Sampaio, C. H. (2019). Antecedents and consequences of impulse buying: a meta-analytic study. RAUSP Management Journal, Vol. 54, No. 2, pp. 178–204.

Sun, T., & Wu, G. (2011). Trait predictors of on-line impulsive buying tendency: A hierarchical approach. Journal of Marketing Theory and Practice, Vol. 19, No. 3, pp. 337–346.

Tifferet, S., & Herstein, R. (2012). Gender differences in brand commitment, impulse buying, and hedonic consumption. Journal of Product & Brand Management., Vol. 21, No. 3, pp. 176–182.

Ward, S., & Wackman, D. B. (1972). Children's purchase influence attempts and parental yielding. Journal of Marketing Research, Vol. 9, No. 3, pp. 316–319.

Xiang, L., Zheng, X., Lee, M. K., & Zhao, D. (2016). Exploring consumers' impulse buying behavior on social commerce platform: the role of parasocial interaction. International Journal of Information Management, Vol. 36, No. 3, pp. 333–347.

Youn, S., & Faber, R. J. (2000). Impulse buying: its relation to personality traits and cues. Advances in Consumer Research, Vol. 27, No. 1, pp. 179–185.

Yu, C., & Bastin, M. (2010). Hedonic shopping value and impulse buying behavior in transitional economies: a symbiosis in the Mainland China marketplace. Journal of Brand Management, Vol. 18, No. 2, pp. 105–114.

CHAPTER 8

PC-based Versus Mobile-Based On-line Shopping

Abstract On-line shopping differs when the device used is a personal computer or a mobile. This aspect deserves attention, especially when talking about impulse buying. The chapter intends to highlight such differences, bringing to light that personal computers allows a more thoughtful approach to purchase. Within the framework of the study (Chap. 10), this is quite important, as an impulse purchase concluded through a PC is the result of more actual convictions, being less affected by situational factors.

Keywords PC-based on-line shopping • Mobile-based on-line shopping • Situational factors • Impulse buying

The aptitude toward on-line shopping can constitute a significant part of the individual's lifestyle, which is substantiated by the carrying out of activities and the nurturing of related interests (Li et al. 1999). For example, Vijayasarathy and Jones (2000) identified seven types of shopping orientation: (1) home shoppers, who mainly buy from home; (2) economic shoppers, who go around the shops before finalizing their choice; (3) mall shoppers, who prefer shopping malls or department stores; (4) personalized shoppers, who prefer to buy in the stores where they know the sellers; (5) ethical shoppers, who enjoy shopping in nearby stores to promote the well-being of the local community; (6) convenience

© The Author(s), under exclusive license to Springer Nature
Switzerland AG 2021
G. Mattia et al., *Online Impulse Buying and Cognitive Dissonance*,
https://doi.org/10.1007/978-3-030-65923-3_8

shoppers, who pay attention to the convenience of shopping; (7) enthusiastic shoppers, who simply buy for the sake of it.

Their results showed that home shoppers have a stronger tendency to buy on-line, the opposite of what happens to mall shoppers. Numerous studies have also shown that the type of shopping orientation is linked to the intention to shop on-line (Ha et al. 2002; Seock 2003; Gehrt et al. 2007). Since e-shopping can occur in different places (home, work, other) without the need to move, it can also be associated with mental, psychological, and economic energy-saving connected to the completion of the purchase.

Therefore, since the web is accessible through different devices (PC, smartphone, tablet), it is relevant to understand how they differ in the management of on-line purchases and in facilitating the purchase intention. With particular regard to PCs and smartphones, there are elements of similarity and others of diversity: both are characterized by the immediacy of access to the same information, while the browsing experience differs, as PCs have larger screens, but have, although laptops, less portability, and therefore a less agile use. Moreover, it is also necessary to focus attention on the different search costs of the two devices. As consumers can easily find even hard-to-find products, on-line shopping puts the consumer in front of large number of choices, much more than physical shopping. However, in the case of PCs, this enormous variety of alternatives can be better managed thanks to the size of the screen, which allows for easier and wider scrolling, while for smartphones this possibility is eliminated, thus increasing search costs. Some authors (Yang and Ghose 2010; Baye and Morgan 2009) have pointed out that the sites better placed in the ranking of appearance during a search have a better chance of being opened when using a PC (primacy effect), especially if someone is using a "comparator" website (Brynjolfsson et al. 2010). This situation has to do with the search costs, which therefore enhance when the screen is smaller, as it creates more difficulty in navigating, understanding, and evaluating information (Chae and Kim 2004), as well as a reduced learning opportunity and a poorer user experience (Shankar et al. 2010; Maniar et al. 2008), unless the sites are adapted to mobile viewing (Adipat et al. 2011).

Another aspect to consider is the reduction of physical and social distance. When a physical store is difficult to reach, the value and importance of the on-line environment increases (Anderson et al. 2010; Forman et al. 2009). However, there is a difference between PC and mobile. In the case of the PC, the reduction of distance has less influence, in the sense that searches are less tied to proximity. More and more often, in fact, search engines return results related to points of interest, based on the keywords that the user has typed. Consequently, the mobile device is the one most elective in these cases (Blum and Goldfarb 2006), as well as with regard to social interactions (Wellman et al. 2002).

It is necessary at this point to understand the differences, in terms of impulsiveness in purchases, produced by the PC compared to the smartphone. It should be reiterated that the on-line environment favors exploration and therefore relates to the impulsiveness of consumers (Ailawadi et al. 2001), especially when this activity produces excitement and fun while observing a product. Since the smartphone is a highly portable device (Okazaki and Mendez 2013), and therefore on average is more used than the PC for recreational activities (especially shopping, news, music, videos), it exposes consumers more to advertising and promotional messages from the various sources consulted (Kourouthanassis and Giaglis 2012). However, there are divergent positions in the literature on the use of the smartphone in on-line shopping: some scholars highlight the advantages linked to the speed of research and the improvement of the quality of decisions (Murray and Häubl 2008; Häubl and Trifts 2000), while others stress elements of distraction, which lead to the reduction of cognitive and decision-making skills (Sciandra and Inman 2013; Hyman et al. 2010). A Rackspace study (2012) found that 17% of surveyed consumers believed that smartphones increased their impulse purchases. This was because of the ease and speed with which a transaction could be made. However, the same research found that about 97% of e-shoppers leave the shopping cart, that is, place products in the shopping cart without completing the transaction. In this regard, researchers assume that consumers are blocked by security issues (e.g. fear of spreading information about their credit card), usability problems, and slow navigation. But another reason is that attributable to a transfer mechanism from one device to another: more precisely, consumers search on smartphones and then buy using the computer. To confirm this hypothesis, they say that on average 2.6 devices are used for each transaction, so smartphone–PC integration is typical of the e-commerce phenomenon.

This thesis suggests that the PC would predispose to a greater caution in purchases, as the situational factors of influence, especially time and speed, typical of smartphone users are less intense. It is, therefore, reasonable to hypothesize that the impulse purchase made through the PC, being less subject to environmental conditions, has a sort of greater purity, that is to say, it comes from the real willingness of consumers.

REFERENCES

Adipat, B., Zhang, D., & Zhou, L. (2011). The effects of tree-view based presentation adaptation on mobile web browsing. Mis Quarterly, pp. 99–121.

Ailawadi, K.L., Neslin, S.A., & Gedenk, K. (2001). Pursuing the value-conscious consumer: store brands versus national brand promotions. Journal of Marketing, Vol. 65, No. 1, pp. 71–89.

Anderson, A. A., Brossard, D., & Scheufele, D. A. (2010). The changing information environment for nanotechnology: On-line audiences and content. Journal of Nanoparticle Research, Vol. 12, No. 4, pp. 1083–1094.

Baye, M. R., & Morgan, J. (2009). Brand and price advertising in on-line markets. Management Science, Vol. 55, No. 7, pp. 1139–1151.

Blum, B. S., & Goldfarb, A. (2006). Does the internet defy the law of gravity? Journal of International Economics, Vol. 70, No. 2, pp. 384–405.

Brynjolfsson, E., Hu, Y., & Smith, M. D. (2010). Research commentary—long tails vs. superstars: the effect of information technology on product variety and sales concentration patterns. Information Systems Research, Vol. 21, No. 4, pp. 736–747.

Chae, M., & Kim, J. (2004). Do size and structure matter to mobile users? An empirical study of the effects of screen size, information structure, and task complexity on user activities with standard web phones. Behaviour & Information Technology, Vol. 23, No. 3, pp. 165–181.

Forman, C., Ghose, A., & Goldfarb, A. (2009). Competition between local and electronic markets: how the benefit of buying on-line depends on where you live. Management Science, Vol. 55, No. 1, pp. 47–57.

Gehrt, K. C., Onzo, N., Fujita, K., & Rajan, M. N. (2007). The emergence of internet shopping in Japan: identification of shopping orientation-defined segments. Journal of Marketing Theory and Practice, Vol. 15, No. 2, pp. 167–177.

Ha, S. H., Bae, S. M., & Park, S. C. (2002). Customer's time-variant purchase behavior and corresponding marketing strategies: an on-line retailer's case. Computers & Industrial Engineering, Vol. 43, No. 4, pp. 801–820.

Häubl, G., & Trifts, V. (2000). Consumer decision making in on-line shopping environments: the effects of interactive decision aids. Marketing Science, Vol. 19, No. 1, pp. 4–21.

Hyman Jr., I. E., Boss, S. M., Wise, B. M., McKenzie, K. E., & Caggiano, J. M. (2010). Did you see the unicycling clown? Inattentional blindness while walking and talking on a cell phone. Applied Cognitive Psychology, Vol. 24, No. 5, pp. 597–607.

Kourouthanassis, P. E., & Giaglis, G. M. (2012). Introduction to the special issue mobile commerce: the past, present, and future of mobile commerce research. International Journal of Electronic Commerce, Vol. 16, No. 4, pp. 5–18.

Li, H., Kuo, C., & Rusell, M. G. (1999). The impact of perceived channel utilities, shopping orientations, and demographics on the consumer's on-line buying behavior. Journal of Computer-Mediated Communication, Vol. 5, No. 2, JCMC521.

Maniar, N., Bennett, E., Hand, S., & Allan, G. (2008). The effect of mobile phone screen size on video-based learning. Journal of Software, Vol. 3, No. 4, pp. 51–61.

Murray, K. B., & Häubl, G. (2008). Interactive consumer decision aids. In: Wierenga, B., Handbook of marketing decision models. New York, NY: Springer Science & Business Media, LLC.

Okazaki, S., & Mendez, F. (2013). Exploring convenience in mobile commerce: Moderating effects of gender. Computers in Human Behavior, Vol. 29, No. 3, pp. 1234–1242.

Rackspace (2012), Tablets and smartphones may increase UK consumer impulse buys by up to £1.1 billion per year, indicates Rackspace retail research. https://www.rackspace.com/en-gb/newsroom/tablets-smartphones-may-increase-uk-consumer-impulse-buys-1-1-billion-per-year-indicates-rackspace-retail-research [Last accessed: March 15, 2020].

Sciandra, M., & Inman, J. (2013). Smart phones, bad decisions? The impact of in-store mobile technology use on consumer decisions. in NA - Advances in Consumer Research Vol. 41, eds. Simona Botti and Aparna Labroo, Duluth, MN: Association for Consumer Research.

Seock, Y. K. (2003). Analysis of clothing websites for young customer retention based on a model of customer relationship management via the internet (Doctoral dissertation, Virginia Tech).

Shankar, V., Hofacker, C., Venkatesh, A., & Naik, P. (2010). Mobile Marketing in the Retailing Environment: Current Insights and Future Research Avenues. Journal of Interactive Marketing, 24(2), pp. 111–120.

Vijayasarathy, L. R., & Jones, J. M. (2000). Intentions to shop using internet catalogues: exploring the effects of product types, shopping orientations, and attitudes towards computers. Electronic Markets, Vol. 10, No. 1, pp. 29–38.

Wellman, B., Boase, J., & Chen, W. (2002). The networked nature of community: on-line and offline. It & Society, Vol. 1, No. 1, pp. 151–165.

Yang, S., & Ghose, A. (2010). Analyzing the relationship between organic and sponsored search advertising: positive, negative, or zero interdependence? Marketing Science, Vol. 29, No. 4, pp. 602–623.

CHAPTER 9

Millennials and On-line Shopping: The Case of Smartphones

Abstract In this chapter Millennials, the target of the study (Chap. 10), are described, in terms of personal and social characteristics, and purchase behavior. This generation has been chosen due to their familiarity with technology and the aptitude toward hedonistic products and experiential consumptions. To better focus their peculiarities, a comparison among other generations over time has been provided.

Keywords Millennials • Generation Y • Experiential consumptions • Hedonistic products

The Millennials, also known as Generation Y, identify all those who reached adulthood in the twenty-first century (Table 9.1). The identification of the age group relative to the Millennials has had multiple definitions over time. For some authors, Millennials are the generation following the so-called Generation X, while for others it is an alternative to identify digital natives, that is, the generation of those born and grown up in correspondence with the spread of new information technologies (Vodanovich et al. 2010; Twenge 2006), having been born and raised in a connected environment that enabled them to use the Internet to access information, products, and other resources anywhere and at any time (Lenhart et al. 2010). The term "Millennials" was coined by Howe and Strauss (1992) to identify all the people born between 1982 and 2004. Gurau (2012)

© The Author(s), under exclusive license to Springer Nature   61
Switzerland AG 2021
G. Mattia et al., *Online Impulse Buying and Cognitive Dissonance*,
https://doi.org/10.1007/978-3-030-65923-3_9

G. MATTIA ET AL.

Table 9.1 Intergenerational differences

	Baby boomer (1940–59)	Gen X (1960–79)	Gen Y (1980–94)	Gen Z (1995–2010)
Historical facts	Vietnam Woodstock Civil rights movements Watergate Space exploration	Fall of the Berlin Wall MTV Foundation of Europe	9/11 terrorist attacks Development of Google, Facebook Video games Euro as a single currency in European countries	Economic downturn Global warming Energy crisis Arab Spring Mixed marriage Rise of populism Brexit
Communication media	Formal letter	Telephone	Email and text	Social media and audio messages
Technology use	Difficult	Uncertain	Can't work without	Digital native
Aspiration	Job security	Security and stability	Work–life balance	Freedom and flexibility

Source: Author's elaboration

stated that Millennials are the individuals born between 1980 and 2000, while Noble et al. (2009) consider the period between 1977 and 1994. According to Ordun (2015), however, the time span in which to consider this generation is 1981–2000. It is possible to note that the differences between the time spans defined in the reported studies are in a range of 20 years (1980–2000).

The representation emerging from the literature on Millennials is that of a generation projected toward adulthood with a series of socio-economic contingencies. This generation grew up following specific mantras such as "follow your dreams" and then found themselves facing a reality with few possibilities for the realization of personal aspirations, due to several economic crises (Hartman and McCambridge 2011). Furlong (2013) described the individuals of this generation as optimistic, committed, participative, competitive, and strongly inclined to teamwork. Burstein (2013) defined their approach to social change as a pragmatic idealism, with "a deep desire to make the world a better place combined with an understanding that doing so requires building new institutions while working inside and outside existing institutions" (p. 3). At the same time, as Laize and Pougnet (2007) pointed out, Millennials are greedy for novelty. Both in their professional and private lives, the exponents of this generation avoid routine and restrictions, and constantly seek new stimuli to respond to their needs. They plan to look for jobs that give them the opportunity to learn and grow, without any fear of the uncertainty of change. On the contrary, according to Chaminade (2007), they like changes in both brands and jobs, because they thrive on ambiguity and uncertainty.

Millennials are more attentive consumers than their predecessors and have very specific buying habits aimed at saving money (Bucic et al. 2012). They spend less and are mainly dedicated to a more selective shopping (Mangold and Smith 2012). Those who can save money do not prefer to buy a house because they are interested in activities such as travel and low-cost holidays (Lenhart et al. 2010). Millennials use the internet to find out which is the best product, the best point of sale, or the best price according to their needs, but afterward they prefer to be able to touch the product and have a direct experience.

The Millennials are recognizable by some specific prerogatives. For example, the predisposition to social connection and familiarity with technology often translates into the role of early adopters and strong web users (Hwang and Griffiths 2017). Given their technological aptitude, this cohort of consumers is characterized by a remarkable familiarity with devices such as smartphones, PCs, digital cameras, much more marked than previous generations (Jones et al. 2010), as well as the aptitude to use the internet for sharing, interaction, and collaboration activities (Burhanna et al. 2009). They have a conception of human relationships largely influenced by IT and digital tools. The Millennials' use of technology and social media strongly influences their behavior in many fields, with the consequence that it can produce positive but even negative effects (Aksoy et al. 2013).

Millennials are strongly interested in experiential consumption—toward which the propensity to spend increases—and social consumption. In fact, they are more inclined to share and talk about their purchases on social channels with their peers (eMarketer 2010), rather than relying on indiscriminate brand loyalty. For these individuals, brand loyalty is optional, because they shift their preferences extemporaneously, unless the brand be able to maintain an incentive and personalized communication.

Trying to compare the Millennials with the generation Z, which follows them from a temporal point of view, some differences appear. It is necessary to make a premise: there are no clear or genetic divisions between one generation and another, but these comparisons are useful methods to read and codify groups of people that differ not only in age, but also in social, economic, and political factors. These generations differ in chronological limits, but also because they have been able to experience some of the most important events in history in different ages.

The Millennials are old enough to have witnessed the attack on the Twin Towers on September 11, 2001, but also to have seen and lived through the crisis and economic recession of 2008. When the iPhone appeared on the market (2007), the members of Generation Z were just 10 years old, while the Millennials had already used first mobile phones and then moved on to mobile phones with the first touchscreen models. Millennials witnessed the computer revolution, while Generation Z was born in a world where the internet established the canons of a new way of life and learned to use it from an early age (Dimock 2019). In fact, some scholars define this generation as digital natives (Turner 2015). As a result, the former had a very close relationship with the internet, from which they drew autonomously and with familiarity to learn (Francis and Hoefel 2018). It is therefore a generation that knows no barriers of connection and therefore, as we had to say before with the Millennials, not even particular limits in its cultural horizons (Gutfreund 2016). Generation Z has never done a school research using only paper encyclopedias, unlike the Millennials that, probably, already in primary school could not use the Web (McHaney 2012).

One of the main consequences of the relationship with the Web for Generation Z is the adoption of different technologies and devices at the same time. Their attention threshold is very low, as they are accustomed to receive many different stimuli at the same time. These evidences also appear in the Millennials, but to a lesser extent.

The individuals of Generation Z believe in themselves and aspire to become entrepreneurs, self-employed (Williams 2015). In contrast, the Millennials want economic certainties and contractual stability as employees, without thinking of becoming self-employed. Furthermore, Millennials tend to be lazy (De Hauw and De Vos 2010). The members of Generation Z are also very independent in their interpersonal relationships, whereas Millennials are often more related to their families.

With regard to the adoption of smartphones, a research by Nielsen (2016) showed that in the United States these devices have reached a total market penetration: the Millennials in 98% of the cases possess a smartphone, followed by 96% of the X Generation. Therefore, the marketing strategies adopted by companies, even in on-line commerce, must adapt their communication and sales activities according to these characteristics and differences between generations.

The process of purchasing a smartphone requires the individual to consider several characteristics before making the final choice (Haba et al. 2017), which are evaluated simultaneously during the purchase process in order to choose the best alternative (Leppaniemi and Karjaluoto 2005): (1) operating system, (2) design, (3) performance, (4) camera quality, (5) battery life, (6) memory, (7) brand, (8) price, (9) display size, (10) weight and dimensions. It is, therefore, necessary to prioritize the selection process. In this respect, several authors have developed studies whose results are substantially convergent. According to Karjaluoto et al. (2005), price, brand, and graphical interface have a significant impact on the purchasing decision. For younger audiences (under 20 years of age), design and size matter most (Hwang and Salvendy 2007). Linked to the relationship between the operating system and design, Mack and Sharples (2009) showed that usability is the most relevant aspect, as also noted by Saif and Wahid (2017), which combined this feature with technological modernity. Bojei and Hoo (2012) introduced the reliable quality of the brand, which was later confirmed by Das et al. (2012), who connected the brand image with the value of an attractive design.

Smartphones have been described as products of hedonistic and interactive technology, which can help to represent the social status of the individuals who own them (Shin et al. 2012). Consequently, the self-representation reflection of a smartphone can be considered as a relevant purchasing factor (Lin and Bhattacherjee 2010). Precisely for this reason, the purchase of a smartphone can be classified among impulse purchases since the consumer also projects feelings and emotions with emotional value on the object. Impulse purchases, in fact, are more related to the concept of luxury and self-gratification rather than to terms such as necessity and functionality. For most consumers, status products are in fact indicators of well-being and affirmation.

The possession of a smartphone does not only depend on the age group and gender; however, the way in which the mobile phone is used can be explained, at least at a first stage, by such variables. As far as the distinction by gender is concerned, the use of mobile phones by females tends to be geared toward the use of social networks, while for males the use is more focused on gaming. Obviously, the discourse changes when moving between different age groups: for example, adults tend to prefer voice calls because of their synchronicity, while younger people prefer communication through social networks (Sanchez-Martínez and Otero 2009). In the case of teenagers, girls tend to use their smartphone as a security measure and use it to control their autonomy, while boys use the phone to demonstrate their independence and to keep up with the times (Igarashi et al. 2005). Another case related to culture and age (different nationality and older age) occurs in some countries where, for example, women use the mobile phone more than men precisely because they have less freedom of movement. Likewise, adults, unlike younger people, do not tend to personalize the device, perhaps because they come from a different generation where the need to establish an identity is a phase that has been overcome, and they are not entirely unacquainted with the use of mobile phones as a symbol of status and identity, unless under given situations: for example, when professionals aspire to leadership positions, mobile phones are used to strengthen their image with customers or corporate membership.

Consumers, thanks to the extensive information available on-line, understand which models are the most appropriate based on their needs. An analysis conducted by Idealo (2018) also tried to understand if there is a direct correlation between the type of mobile phone and the consumer's propensity to spend (more or less) to get it. The four most desired brands in 2018 were analyzed: Apple (25.4%, percentage that concerns the purchase intentions in the Smartphone category), Huawei (slightly lower at 22.3%), Samsung (19.4%), and Xiaomi (7.8%). The most interesting result obtained through the research is related to the analysis of smartphone buyers, divided into age groups, and in relation to their attachment to a specific brand. The results provide information about teenagers, who tend to be most attracted to more flashy brands: in this case Apple and Samsung. Young people feel the need to be represented by the device, which has the task to act as a symbol, in order to make the buyer feel part of a reference group. Differently, adults tend to buy mobile phones equally well, but belonging to less famous and luxurious brands, such as Huawei and Xiaomi: in fact, these users prefer to spend less on a mobile phone that has the same features as another one that costs twice as much. It is therefore possible to affirm that the motivations pushing consumers to buy a smartphone are different and vary according to subject, culture, age, gender, and country (Srivastava 2005).

In light of what has been said so far, the purchasing behavior of Millennials must also be assessed taking into account cultural and psychological aspects, which are key elements in understanding intergenerational differences. More in detail, the specificities of Millennials relate to greater social and parental protection, and greater social propensity, favoring a lifestyle that is less affected by stress. The role of technology, in this framework, assumes a socializing value, and technological products are privileged among the top brands, toward which there is a greater willingness to spend, especially using on-line channels. Suffice it to say that 54% of Millennials make purchases on-line and that the smartphone is a privileged means of purchase in 63% of cases (UPS 2016).

The smartphone for this target is a tool with functional and expressive values of particular importance, whose purchase deserves therefore to be better understood from the point of view of impulsiveness and the consequent risk of cognitive dissonance. For this purpose, in the following chapter, the results of a research in which three different and connected constructs—impulsiveness, cognitive dissonance, and affect state at the time of purchase—are presented, aimed at ascertaining whether the mood acts as moderator between an impulse buying and the onset of the consequent cognitive dissonance.

REFERENCES

Aksoy, L., Van Riel, A., Kandampully, J., Bolton, R. N., Parasuraman, A., Hoefnagels, A., & Solnet, D. (2013). Understanding Generation Y and their use of social media: a review and research agenda. Journal of Service Management. Vol. 24, No. 3, pp. 245–267.

Bojei, J., & Hoo, W. C. (2012). Brand equity and current use as the new horizon for repurchase intention of smartphone. International Journal of Business & Society, Vol. 13, No. 1, pp. 33 – 48.

Bucic, T., Harris, J., & Arli, D. (2012). Ethical consumers among the millennials: a cross-national study. Journal of Business Ethics, Vol. 110, No. 1, pp. 113–131.

Burhanna, K. J., Seeholzer, J., & Salem Jr, J. (2009). No natives here: a focus group study of student perceptions of Web 2.0 and the academic library. The Journal of Academic Librarianship, Vol. 35, No. 6, pp. 523–532.

Burstein, D. (2013). Fast future: how the Millennial generation is shaping our world. Boston: Beacon Press.

Chaminade, B. (2007). Comprendre et manager la Génération Y. In: Journal du Net. Available at http://www.journaldunet.com/management/0705/0705188-generation-y.shtml [Last accessed: 07/07/2020].

Das, G., Datta, B., & Guin, K. K. (2012). Impact of retailer personality on consumer-based retailer equity. Asia Pacific Journal of Marketing and Logistics, Vol. 24, No. 4, pp. 619–639.

De Hauw, S., & De Vos, A. (2010). Millennials' career perspective and psychological contract expectations: does the recession lead to lowered expectations? Journal of Business and Psychology. Vol. 25, No. 2, pp. 293–302.

Dimock, M. (2019). Defining generations: where Millennials end and Generation Z begins. Pew Research Center, Vol. 17, pp. 1–7.

Francis, T., & Hoefel, F. (2018). True Gen: generation Z and its implications for companies. McKinsey & Company.

Furlong, A. (2013). Youth studies: an introduction. New York: Routledge.

Gurau, C. (2012). A life-stage analysis of consumer loyalty profile: comparing generation X and millennial consumers. Journal of Consumer Marketing, Vol. 29, No. 2, pp. 103–113.

Gutfreund, J. (2016). Move over, Millennials: generation Z is changing the consumer landscape. Journal of Brand Strategy, Vol. 5, No. 3, pp. 245–249.

Haba, H., Hassan, Z., & Dastane, O. (2017). Factors leading to consumer perceived value of smartphones and its impact on purchase intention. Global Business and Management Research: an International Journal, Vol. 9, No. 1, pp. 42–71.

Hartman, J. L., McCambridge, J. (2011). Optimizing millennials' communication styles. Business Communication Quarterly, Vol. 74, No. 1, pp. 22–44.

Hwang, J., & Griffiths, M. A. (2017). Share more, drive less: millennials value perception and behavioral intent in using collaborative consumption services. Journal of Consumer Marketing. Vol. 32, No. 2, pp. 132–146.

Hwang, W., & Salvendy, G. (2007). What makes evaluators to find more usability problems? A meta-analysis for individual detection rates. In: International conference on human-computer interaction (pp. 499–507). Springer, Berlin, Heidelberg.

Howe, N., & Strauss, W. (1992). Generations: The History of America's Future, 1584 to 2069. Perennial, Harper Collins Publishers.

Idealo (2018). L'e-commerce in Italia: Le nuove abitudini di acquisto on-line. Available at https://www.idealo.it/magazine/wpcontent/uploads/sites/32/2018/03/2018_ebook_ecommerce_idealo_scarica_gratis_IT.pdf [Last accessed: 7 July, 2020].

Igarashi, T., Takai, J., & Yoshida, T. (2005). Gender differences in social network development via mobile phone text messages: A longitudinal study. Journal of Social and Personal Relationships, Vol. 22, No. 5, pp. 691–713.

Jones, C., Ramanau, R., Cross, S., & Healing, G. (2010). Net generation or digital natives: is there a distinct new generation entering university? Computers & Education, Vol. 54, No. 3, pp. 722–732.

Karjaluoto, H., Karvonen, J., Kesti, M., Koivumäki, T., Manninen, M., Pakola, J., & Salo, J. (2005). Factors affecting consumer choice of mobile phones: two studies from Finland. Journal of Euromarketing, Vol. 14, No. 3, pp. 59–82.

Laize, C., & Pougnet, S. (2007). Un modèle de développement des compétences sociales et relationnelles des jeunes d'aujourd'hui et managers de demain. Fribourg: XVIIIème congrès de l'AGRH.

Lenhart, A., Ling, R., Campbell, S., & Purcell, K. (2010). Teens and mobile phones: text messaging explodes as teens embrace it as the centerpiece of their communication strategies with friends. Pew Internet & American Life Project.

Leppaniemi, M., & Karjaluoto, H. (2005). Factors influencing consumers' willingness to accept mobile advertising: a conceptual model. International Journal of Mobile Communications, Vol. 3, No. 3, pp. 197–213.

Lin, C. P., & Bhattacherjee, A. (2010). Extending technology usage models to interactive hedonic technologies: a theoretical model and empirical test. Information Systems Journal, Vol. 20, No. 2, pp. 163–181.

Mack, Z., & Sharples, S. (2009). The importance of usability in product choice: a mobile phone case study. Ergonomics, Vol. 52, No. 12, pp. 1514–1528.

Mangold, W. G., & Smith, K. T. (2012). Selling to Millennials with on-line reviews. Business Horizons, Vol. 55, No. 2, pp. 141–153.

McHaney, R. (2012). The new digital shoreline: how Web 2.0 and millennials are revolutionizing higher education. Stylus Publishing, LLC.

Nielsen (2016). Millennials are top smartphone users. http://www.nielsen.com/us/en/insights/news/2016/millennials-are-top-smartphone-users.html [Last accessed June 16, 2020].

Noble, S. M., Haytko, D. L., & Phillips, J. (2009). What drives college-age generation Y consumers? Journal of Business Research, Vol. 62, No. 1, pp. 617–628.

Ordun, G. (2015). Millennial (Gen Y) consumer behavior their shopping preferences and perceptual maps associated with brand loyalty. Canadian Social Science, Vol. 11, No. 4, pp. 40–55.

Saif, S. M., & Wahid, A. (2017). Effort estimation techniques for web application development: a review. International journal of Advanced Research in Computer Science, Vol. 8, No. 9, pp. 125–131.

Sánchez-Martínez, M., & Otero, A. (2009). Factors associated with cell phone use in adolescents in the community of Madrid (Spain). Cyber Psychology & Behavior, Vol. 12, No. 2, pp. 131–137.

Shin, C., Hong, J. H., & Dey, A. K. (2012). Understanding and prediction of mobile application usage for smart phones. In: Proceedings of the 2012 ACM Conference on Ubiquitous Computing, pp. 173–182.

Srivastava, L. (2005). Mobile phones and the evolution of social behaviour. Behaviour & Information Technology, pp. 111–129.

Turner, A. (2015). Generation Z: technology and social interest. The Journal of Individual Psychology, 71(2), 103–113.

Twenge, J. (2006). Generation me: why today's young Americans are more confident, assertive, entitled – and more miserable than ever before. New York: Free Press Simon and Schuster.

UPS (2016). UPS Pulse of the On-line Shopper. Available at https://pressroom.ups.com/assets/pdf/2016_UPS_Pulse%20of%20the%20On-line%20Shopper_executive%20summary_final.pdf [Last accessed: June 16, 2020].

Vodanovich, S., Sundaram, D., & Myers, M. (2010). Research commentary-digital natives and ubiquitous information systems. Information Systems Research, Vol. 21, No. 4, pp. 711–723.

Williams, A. (2015). Move over, millennials, here comes Generation Z. The New York Times, Vol. 18.

CHAPTER 10

The Study

Abstract The purpose of this chapter is to present the results of an empirical study, carried out through a quantitative survey, testing two main hypotheses: (1) to verify whether an impulse buying of a smartphone via an e-commerce marketplace affects the onset of cognitive dissonance and (2) to verify whether the positive affective state accompanying the impulse buying under the first hypothesis moderates the onset of cognitive dissonance. Results, conclusion, and implications are discussed in the final part of the chapter.

Keywords Quantitative survey • Moderation analysis

INTRODUCTION

The past 60 years have witnessed an increasing interest in the comprehension of the impulse buying behavior (Peck and Childers 2006; Rook 1987; Stern 1962; Clover 1950). In 2014, it was estimated that in the US

This chapter presents the results of a research conducted and presented at the ICHCBDP 2020: XIV International Conference on Hospitality Consumer Behavior and Decision Process, Barcelona, on February 10–11, where it was granted the Best Paper Award.

© The Author(s), under exclusive license to Springer Nature
Switzerland AG 2021
G. Mattia et al., *Online Impulse Buying and Cognitive Dissonance*,
https://doi.org/10.1007/978-3-030-65923-3_10

market impulse purchases grew up by 50% compared to 2010 (Chang and Tseng 2014).

The nature of impulse buying "can stimulate emotional conflict. In addition, it is prone to occur with a minor regard for its consequences" (Rook and Fisher 1995). Recent studies (Luna and Quintanilla 2000) have shown that impulse buying is mainly affective and emotional and determine consumer behavior to a greater extent than utilitarian and rational aspects.

Therefore, it can be assumed that impulse buyers could experience post-purchase anxiety due to the emerging doubts on the appropriateness of the choice made—for instance, as an effect of ignored characteristics of the product (Chang and Tseng 2014)—the so-called cognitive dissonance (Festinger 1957). However, it is legitimate to wonder whether a post-purchase cognitive dissonance arises only from betrayed expectations or the understated purchase consequences. From this perspective, the role of a positive affect state may act as a moderator of cognitive dissonance. In fact, when a consumer is in "good mood", it may be less prone to consider its impulse purchase with excessive criticism, thus reducing the impact of its regret.

The present research is aimed at determining whether the positive affect state may moderate the onset of cognitive dissonance after an impulse purchase of a high expressive value such as a smartphone.

The authors consciously limit the scope of the research by considering (1) the purchase via desktop computer through an e-commerce marketplace (2) as far as the target is concerned, a sample of Millennial individuals. The research is deemed relevant for (1) the considerable increase in purchases through the digital channel and (2) the greater propensity of consumers to make impulse purchases through on-line channels (Kim and Johnson 2011). The results offer insights for the reduction of cognitive dissonance to third parties managing e-commerce platforms.

THEORETICAL BACKGROUND AND HYPOTHESIS

Based on the literature review of previous chapters, an uncertainty emerges on the relation among three dimensions of the purchasing process: (1) the impulse buying, (2) the positive affect state at the time of purchase, and (3) the rise of post-purchase cognitive dissonance.

This study aims to fill such a gap and focuses its scope on the context of on-line shopping of a high expressive value product (smartphone), which may solicit impulse buying due to its hedonistic and functional appeal and for this very reason give rise to the cognitive dissonance. The smartphone has become an important and inseparable tool from the modern life of customers, especially for Millennials. According to eMarketer (2018), the number of smartphone users worldwide will increase from about 2.53 billion by 2018 to more than 2.87 billion by 2020. In the process of purchasing a smartphone, consumers not only consider the quality of products, but are also concerned about the service quality and other aspects such as brand, price, operating system, and screen size. Furthermore, they tend to attribute the smartphone a symbolic power, able to enhance the extended self of the individual.

The research investigates the phenomenon of impulse buying and its relationship with cognitive dissonance. Millennials, the target of the study, include because of their intimate familiarity with digital technologies in areas of communication, education, and information exchange (Connor et al. 2008).

The specific choice of applying this research to Millennials relates to (1) their experience with e-commerce purchases and (2) the propensity toward products with expressive and hedonistic value (Shah et al. 2012) to which smartphones can be ascribed.

Only purchases accomplished via desktop computers were taken into account; despite mobile devices represent an indisputable on-line purchase tool, it can be reasonably assumed that the two differ in terms of purchase behavior (i.e., time spent to compare products and collect information) and deserve a separate discussion.

According to the above statements, we posit the following hypothesis:

H1: Impulse buying of a smartphone via an e-commerce marketplace accomplished through a desktop computer affects the onset of cognitive dissonance.

H2: The positive affective state accompanying the impulse buying under H1 conditions moderates the onset of cognitive dissonance.

Figure 10.1 shows the conceptual model used in the research.

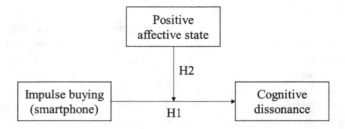

Fig. 10.1 Conceptual model. (Source: Author's elaboration)

Table 10.1 Research steps

ID	Steps	Sample
1	Recruitment of respondents on social channels	$n = 598$
2	Snowballing approach to expand the panel	$n = 702$
3	Selection of impulse buyers with the IBTS scale	$n = 217$
4	Selection of respondents with positive affective state with PANAS scale	$n = 212$
5	Measurement of the cognitive dissonance with Sweeney scale	$n = 212$
6	Moderation analysis on the positive affective state of the person at the time of the impulsive purchase	$n = 212$

Methodology

The measurement of the three constructs under examination—impulse buying tendency, cognitive dissonance, and positive affective state—was performed using three scales: (1) the impulsive buying tendency scale (IBTS) (Verplanken et al. 2005), consisting of 20 items; (2) the Sweeney scale (22 items); and (3) the positive and negative affect scale (PANAS) (Watson et al. 1988) (20 items).

The research design followed several steps (Table 10.1): (1) recruitment on social channels (LinkedIn, Facebook, Instagram) over a period of eight weeks (February–March 2019) of consumers born between 1980 and 1995, who in the previous six months had purchased a smartphone in the price range 200–400 euros. This range was considered compatible with the possibility of an impulse purchase within the target in question; (2) starting from the individuals that responded to the survey ($n = 598$), the sample was expanded with a snowballing approach, reaching a total of 702 units (+103); (3) selection of eligible individuals carried out through a specific questionnaire with the IBTS scale, with the aim at selecting only the impulse buyers (grade 4–5 in the interval 1–5), which produced a new sample of 271; (4) distribution of a questionnaire to the above sample with the PANAS scale to identify respondents with positive affective state ($n = 212$) at the time of the impulse purchase; (5) administration of the Sweeney scale to the sample thus obtained to measure the cognitive dissonance; (6) verification of the research hypothesis through a moderation analysis, in order to demonstrate whether the positive affect state of the person at the time of the impulsive purchase exert an effect on the cognitive dissonance. The test was carried out using the Hayes macro (Process), through the SPSS software.

Moderation analysis is used to test the effect of an independent variable on a dependent one when it is assumed that a third exogenous variable (the so-called moderation variable) moderates (influences) the relationship between them. When this happens, an interaction effect is produced. To test the moderation effect, a standard regression model (the so-called moderate regression) is used, calculating the regression coefficient of the independent variable, that of the independent moderation variable, and finally the combined regression coefficients of the two. The single effect of the two independent variables is referred to as first order, whereas the second order refers to the combined effect of the two.

RESULTS AND DISCUSSION

Prior to the verification of the hypothesis, descriptive statistics were carried out on the sample investigated aimed at its profiling (see Table 10.2): sex ($M = 60\%$; $F = 40\%$), age groups (20–30 = 60%; 31–40 = 40%), gross annual disposable income (lower than 20,000 = 45%; 20,000–40,000 = 40%; above 40,000 = 15%), and job (student = 26%; employee: 46%; freelance: 19%; other 9%). Of the sample, 68% bought a smartphone in the price

Table 10.2 Sample demographics

Symbol	Quantity	%
Gender	Male: 127; female: 85	Male: 60%; female: 40%
Age	20–30: 127; 31–40: 85	21–30: 60%; 31–40: 40%
Income (€)	< 20 k: 95; 20–40 k: 85; > 40 k: 32	< 20 k: 45%; 20–40 k: 40%; > 40 k: 15%;
Job	Student: 56; employee: 98; freelance: 39; other: 19	Student: 26%; employee: 46%; freelance: 19%; other: 9%

range of € 200–300 and 32% in the price range of € 300–400. Subsequently, a chi-square independence test was performed, using the availability of income and the price range of the smartphone as tabulation variables. The test revealed ($p < 0.05$) the dependence between the two characters, showing that the impulsive purchase is valid for a product whose price is related to economic availability. The intensity of the association between the characters, calculated with the phi index, was equal to 0.327.

Moving on to the moderation analysis, the internal consistency of the three scales was measured through Cronbach's alpha coefficient, which returned the following values (IBTS: 0.89; PANAS: 0.91; Sweeney: 0.87). The convergent validity of the scales was verified according to average variance extracted—AVE—and composite reliability—CR—with the following results: IBTS: AVE: 0.701; CR: 0.820; PANAS: AVE: 0.612; CR: 0.799; Sweeney: AVE: 0.699; CR: 0.812. The data are above the thresholds deemed adequate to affirm the reliability and validity of the constructs: 0.7 for Cronbach's alpha (Nunnally 1978); 0.5 for AVE and 0.7 for CR (Fornell and Larcker 1981).

The authors then proceeded to test the system of relationships of the moderation scheme, with the aim of verifying whether the impulse purchase and the affect state contextual to it interacted in the onset of cognitive dissonance. From the analysis it emerged that (1) the adjusted coefficient of determination of the model was equal to 0.432, with test F significant ($p < 0.05$); (2) the coefficient of regression of the impulse purchase on the cognitive dissonance was equal to 0.524 ($p < 0.05$); (3) the coefficient of regression of the positive affective state on cognitive dissonance was equal to -0.322 ($p < 0.05$); (4) the interaction effect of the two independent variables (impulse purchase and positive affective state) on cognitive dissonance is equal to -0.189 (not significant). It can be deduced, therefore, that the positive affect state does not moderate the effects of the impulse purchase of a smartphone on the subsequent onset of cognitive dissonance.

As a consequence, H1 is supported, whereas H2 had to be rejected.

CONCLUSION

From the first empirical evidence it is possible to make some early considerations. At first, the lack of moderation of the positive affective state must be contextualized to the product under consideration. The target of the study (Millennial individuals) has a degree of technological competence "naturally" acquired. One can therefore expect that the choice of the smartphone implies a more punctual evaluation, even if subsequent to the purchase, of functional and performance elements, which the impulsive behavior does not primarily consider. Furthermore, the choice is affected by attributes such as design or brand affection, typical of the symbolic value of the product. Second, the influence that digital platforms can exert on impulse buying should be noted. As reported by the literature (Bilgihan 2016) an environment that supports immersive user experience, accompanied by ease, security, and speed of the transaction, can encourage a greater willingness to make an impulse purchase.

Consequently, given that the positive affect state has no influence on the onset of cognitive dissonance, the crucial part of post-purchase management resides on customer support to mitigate the effect of doubts and anxiety. In addition, the management of possible problems/complaints should be coped in order to increase the customer satisfaction and loyalty (Chang and Tseng 2014).

An examination of how temporal antecedents and responses to dissonance vary across contexts could also help explaining why dissonance sometimes yields positive outcomes while at other times producing counterproductive results (Hinojosa et al. 2017). Today, consumers are increasingly having an omnichannel approach that involves a multitude of offline and on-line channels before making a purchase, and the possibility of impulse purchases for certain types of product is large (Sopadjieva et al. 2017). The same goes for cognitive dissonance: even if the purchase is made on-line, the consumer can retrieve information and try out the product at a physical point of sale before buying on-line (Jeong et al. 2019). Therefore, it is important to reconstruct all the touch points along the customer purchase journey to more deeply understand the factors that cause these phenomena.

Accordingly, by reducing cognitive dissonance, consumers could fulfill their expectations and be more inclined to experience satisfaction and loyalty. In this regard, proper information provided by the e-retailer would soak the friction between expected and actual result of a purchase choice. Persuasion, understood as a set of reliable and convincing arguments, when properly used as a communication strategy may help to overlap consumer beliefs and post-purchase attitude, thus relieving the possible condition of frustration and discomfort—the above also considering that emotions exert a remarkable role in the triggering of an impulse purchase. Positive or negative affect states enhance the possibility that an impulse driven individual be subject to a sudden decision: in this case, information becomes a leverage to increase the consciousness of consumers. As highlighted in the previous chapters, cognitive dissonance cannot prevent the repetition of impulse purchases, because impulsivity is related to personality traits and situational factors, as well as to an instinctive tendency to remove the memory of a wrong choice. However, information may solicit consumers to a more thoughtful purchase process. Actually, information represents a lens for an heuristic approach to the choice, preventing cognitive dissonance rather than reducing or neutralizing it after it has already occurred.

Furthermore, on-line impulse buying should represent a first touch point with the new customer and the premise of a lasting relationship. Under this respect, the role of the affective state in the newly presented picture may be inserting positive emotions and reassurance during and after the on-line shopping experience. This point of view is interesting to deepen due to the growing research on omnichannel retail management (Mirsch et al. 2016), which could also include the transition to the point of sale during the entire purchase journey. It is well recognized that in-store marketing activities, capturing shoppers' attention, may lead to unplanned buying (Inman et al. 2009), whereas outside the store, consumers may be more likely to be engaged in planning (Abratt and Goodey 1990).

The effects of shopping factors on on-line purchasing decisions are designed to create a new scenario for marketing professionals. For instance, whenever peer evaluation of a certain purchase choice is deemed as satisfactory, impulse consumers may be less prone to develop cognitive dissonance. Therefore, communication should encourage on-line word of mouth through social networks, blogs, and forums, where consumers could play an active role telling others their shopping experience. Should this condition be accomplished, it can be assumed that the mitigation of cognitive dissonance creates a twofold advantage: on the one hand, less risk of repentance, and on the other an increase in the market performance of the companies involved.

This study has limitations that offer opportunities for further research developments. The generalizability of the results is subject to certain limitations. For instance, limits relate (1) to the use of a non-probabilistic sample; (2) to the distorting effect of the memory effort in contextualizing the state of mind of a purchase made over a relatively long period of time (up to six months); (3) to the lack of distinction between different reasons of use (i.e., primary or secondary smartphones), which may impact on the viability of an impulse behavior; (4) the perception of brands, which may elicit different cognitive/affective attitudes. Eventually, future researches could take into account (1) the study of the same phenomenon applied to mobile devices, in order to assess the extent to which they influence the attitude toward impulsivity; (2) the differentiation among sex and instruction level, which might produce specific behaviors and reactions in terms of impulse buying and cognitive dissonance.

REFERENCES

Abratt, R., & Goodey, S. D. (1990). Unplanned buying and in-store stimuli in supermarkets. Managerial and Decision Economics, 11(2), 111–121.

Bilgihan, A. (2016). Gen Y customer loyalty in on-line shopping: an integrated model of trust, user experience and branding. Computers in Human Behavior, 61, 103–113.

Chang, C., & Tseng, A. (2014). The post-purchase communication strategies for supporting on-line impulsive buying. Computers in Human Behavior, Vol. 39, No. 1, pp. 393–403.

Clover, V. T. (1950). Relative importance of impulse-buying in retail stores. The Journal of Marketing, Vol. 15, No. 1, pp. 66–70.

Connor, H., Shaw, S., & Fairhurst, D. (2008). Engaging a new generation of graduates. Education + Training, Vol. 50, No. 5, pp. 366–378.

eMarketer (2018). Global proximity mobile payment users: eMarketer's estimates for 2016–2021. https://www.emarketer.com/report/global-proximity-mobile-payment-users-emarketers-estimates-20162021/2002187 [Last accessed: July 7, 2020].

Festinger, L. (1957). A theory of cognitive dissonance. Stanford University Press.

Fornell, C., & Larcker, D. F. (1981). Evaluating structural equation models with unobservable variables and measurement error. Journal of Marketing Research, Vol. 18, No. 1, pp. 39–50.

Hinojosa, A. S., Gardner, W. L., Walker, H. J., Cogliser, C., & Gullifor, D. (2017). A review of cognitive dissonance theory in management research: Opportunities for further development. Journal of Management, 43(1), 170–199.

Inman, J. J., Winer, R. S., & Ferraro, R. (2009). The interplay among category characteristics, customer characteristics, and customer activities on in-store decision making. Journal of Marketing, 73(5), 19–29.

Jeong, M., Zo, H., Lee, C. H., & Ceran, Y. (2019). Feeling displeasure from online social media postings: A study using cognitive dissonance theory. Computers in Human Behavior, 97, 231–240.

Luna, R., & Quintanilla, I. (2000). El modelo de compra ACB. Una nueva conceptualizacion de la compra por impulso. Esic Market. Revista Internacional de Economía y Empresa, Vol. 106, No.1, pp. 151–163.

Mirsch, T., Lehrer, C., & Jung, R. (2016). Channel integration towards omnichannel management: a literature review. Conference: Pacific Asia Conference on Information Systems (PACIS). At: Chiayi, Taiwan.

Nunnally, J. C. (1978). Psychometric theory. McGraw-Hill, New York, 2nd Edition.

Peck, J., & Childers, T. L. (2006). If I touch it, I have to have it: individual and environmental influences on impulse purchasing. Journal of Business Research, Vol. 59, No. 6, pp. 765–769.

Rook, D. W. (1987). The Buying Impulse. Journal of Consumer Research, Vol. 14, No. 2, pp. 189–197.

Rook, D. W., & Fisher, R. J. (1995). Normative influences on impulsive buying behavior. Journal of Consumer Research, Vol. 22, No. 3, pp. 305–313.

Shah, M., Guha, S., & Shrivastava, U. (2012). Effect of emerging trends in retail sector on impulse buying behavior. International Journal of Ems., Vol. 3, No. 2.

Sopadjieva, E., Dholakia, U.M., & Benjamin, B. (2017). A Study of 46,000 Shoppers Shows That Omnichannel Retailing Works. Harvard Business Review, January 03.

Stern, H. (1962). The significance of impulse buying today. Journal of Marketing, Vol. 26, No. 2, pp. 59–62.

Verplanken, B., Herabadi, A. G., Perry, J. A., & Silvera, D. H. (2005). Consumer style and health: the role of impulsive buying in unhealthy eating. Psychology and Health, Vol. 20, No. 4, pp. 429–441.

Watson, D., Clark, L. A., & Tellegen, A. (1988). Development and validation of brief measures of positive and negative affect: the PANAS scales. Journal of Personality and Social Psychology, Vol. 54, No. 6, pp. 1063–1070.

References

Abratt, R., & Goodey, S. D. (1990). Unplanned buying and in-store stimuli in supermarkets. Managerial and Decision Economics, 11(2), pp. 111–121.

Adipat, B., Zhang, D., & Zhou, L. (2011). The effects of tree-view based presentation adaptation on mobile web browsing. Mis Quarterly, pp. 99–121.

Ailawadi, K. L., Neslin, S. A., & Gedenk, K. (2001). Pursuing the value-conscious consumer: store brands versus national brand promotions. Journal of marketing, Vol. 65, No. 1, pp. 71–89.

Ajzen, I., 1991. The theory of planned behavior. Organizational behavior and human decision processes, Vol. 50, No. 2, pp. 179–211.

Aksoy, L., Van Riel, A., Kandampully, J., Bolton, R. N., Parasuraman, A., Hoefnagels, A., & Solnet, D. (2013). Understanding Generation Y and their use of social media: a review and research agenda. Journal of Service Management. Vol. 24, No. 3, pp. 245–267.

Amos, C., Holmes, G. R., & Keneson, W. C. (2014). A meta-analysis of consumer impulse buying. Journal of Retailing and Consumer Services, Vol. 21, No. 2, pp. 86–97.

Anderson, A. A., Brossard, D., Scheufele, D. A. (2010). The changing information environment for nanotechnology: On-line audiences and content. Journal of Nanoparticle Research, Vol. 12, No. 4, pp. 1083–1094.

Axsom, D. (1989). Cognitive dissonance and behavior change in psychotherapy. Journal of Personality and Social Psychology. Vol. 25, No. 3, pp. 234–252.

Babin, B., & Harris, E., 2013. CB5. South-Western, Mason, OH.

Babu, G., & Gallayanee, Y. (2010). Impulse buying and cognitive dissonance: A study conducted among the spring break student shoppers. Young Consumers, Vol. 11, pp. 291–306.

© The Author(s), under exclusive licence to Springer Nature Switzerland AG 2021
G. Mattia et al., *Online Impulse Buying and Cognitive Dissonance*,
https://doi.org/10.1007/978-3-030-65923-3

82 REFERENCES

Babu, G., & Manoj, E. (2009). Cognitive Dissonance and Purchase Involvement in the Consumer Behavior Context. Journal of Marketing Management, Vol. 8, No. 3–4, pp. 7–24.

Bakos, Y. (1997). Reducing buyer search costs: implications for electronic marketplaces. Management Science, Vol. 43, No. 12, pp. 1676–1692.

Balcetis, E., & Dunning, D. (2010). Wishful seeing: more desired objects are seen as closer. Psychological Science, Vol. 21, No. 1, pp. 147–152.

Bandura, A. (1977), Social Learning Theory, Prentice Hall, Englewood Cliffs, New Jersey.

Banerjee, R., & Dittmar, H. (2008). Individual differences in children's materialism: The role of peer relations. Personality and Social Psychology Bulletin, Vol. 34, No. 1, pp. 17–31.

Bawa, A., & Kansal, P. (2008). Cognitive dissonance and the marketing of services: Some Issues. Journal of Services Research, Vol. 8, No. 2, pp. 31–51.

Baye, M. R., & Morgan, J. (2009). Brand and price advertising in on-line markets. Management Science, Vol. 55, No. 7, pp. 1139–1151.

Bayley, G., & Nancarrow, C. (1998). Impulse purchasing: a qualitative exploration of the phenomenon. Qualitative Market Research: An International Journal. Vol. 1, No. 2, pp. 99–114.

Beatty, S. E., & Ferrell, M. E. (1998). Impulse buying: Modeling its precursors. Journal of Retailing, Vol. 74, No. 2, pp. 169–191.

Beatty, S. E., & Kahle, L. R. (1988). Alternative hierarchies of the attitude-behavior relationship: the impact of brand commitment and habit. Journal of the Academy of Marketing Science, Vol. 16, No. 2, pp. 1–10.

Beauvois, J.-L., & Joule, R.-V. (2019). A radical point of view on dissonance theory. In E. Harmon-Jones (Ed.), Cognitive dissonance: Reexamining a pivotal theory in psychology (p. 41–61). American Psychological Association.

Beharrell, B., & Denison, T. J. (1995). Involvement in a routine food shopping context. British Food Journal. Vol. 97, No. 4, pp. 24–29.

Bellenger, D. N., Robertson, D. H., & Hirschman, E. C. (1978). Impulse buying varies by product. Journal of Advertising Research, Vol. 18, No. 6, pp. 15–18.

Bellman, S. B. (2012). I would rather be happy than right: consumer impulsivity, risky decision making, and accountability. PhD (Doctor of Philosophy) thesis, University of Iowa.

Bilgihan, A. (2016). Gen Y customer loyalty in on-line shopping: an integrated model of trust, user experience and branding. Computers in Human Behavior, 61, 103–113.

Blackwell, R. D., Miniard, P.-W., & Engel, J. F. (2012). Consumer behavior. 9th edition, Cengage Learning, Asia.

Bless, H., Bohner, G., Schwarz, N., & Strack, F. (1990). Mood and persuasion: A cognitive response analysis. Personality and Social Psychology Bulletin, Vol. 16, No. 2, pp. 331–345.

REFERENCES **83**

Blum, B. S., & Goldfarb, A. (2006). Does the internet defy the law of gravity? Journal of International Economics, Vol. 70, No. 2, pp. 384–405.

Bohner, G., Moskowitz, G. B., & Chaiken, S. (1995). The interplay of heuristic and systematic processing of social information. European Review of Social Psychology, Vol. 6, No. 1, pp. 33–68.

Bojei, J., & Hoo, W. C. (2012). Brand equity and current use as the new horizon for repurchase intention of smartphone. International Journal of Business & Society, Vol. 13, No. 1, pp. 33 – 48.

Bratko, D., Butkovic, A., & Bosnjak, M. (2013). Twin study of impulsive buying and its overlap with personality. Journal of Individual Differences, Vol. 34, pp. 8–1.

Brynjolfsson, E., Hu, Y., & Smith, M. D. (2010). Research commentary—long tails vs. superstars: the effect of information technology on product variety and sales concentration patterns. Information Systems Research, Vol. 21, No. 4, pp. 736–747.

Bucic, T., Harris, J., & Arli, D. (2012). Ethical consumers among the millennials: a cross-national study. Journal of Business Ethics, Vol. 110, No. 1, pp. 113–131.

Burhanna, K. J., Seeholzer, J., & Salem Jr, J. (2009). No natives here: a focus group study of student perceptions of Web 2.0 and the academic library. The Journal of Academic Librarianship, Vol. 35, No. 6, pp. 523–532.

Burstein, D. (2013). Fast future: how the Millennial generation is shaping our world. Boston: Beacon Press.

Cao, Y., Lu, Y., Gupta, S., & Yang, S. (2015). The effects of differences between e-commerce and m-commerce on the consumers' usage transfer from on-line to mobile channel. IJMC, Vol. 13, No. 1, pp. 51–70.

Casaleggio e Associati (2020). E-commerce in Italia, 2020. https://www.casaleggio.it/e-commerce/. [Last accessed: June 16, 2020].

Chae, M., & Kim, J. (2004). Do size and structure matter to mobile users? An empirical study of the effects of screen size, information structure, and task complexity on user activities with standard web phones. Behaviour & information technology, Vol. 23, No. 3, pp. 165–181.

Chaminade, B. (2007). Comprendre et manager la Génération Y. In: Journal du Net. Available at http://www.journaldunet.com/management/0705/0705188-generation-y.shtml [Last accessed: 07/07/2020].

Chang, C., & Tseng, A. (2014). The post-purchase communication strategies for supporting on-line impulsive buying. Computers in Human Behavior, Vol. 39, No. 1, pp. 393–403.

Chang, H. J., Yan, R. N., & Eckman, M. (2014). Moderating effects of situational characteristics on impulse buying. International Journal of Retail & Distribution Management, Vol. 42, No. 4, pp. 298–314.

84 REFERENCES

Chiang, K., & Dholakia, R. R. (2003). Factors driving consumer intention to shop on-line: an empirical investigation. Journal of Consumer Psychology, Vol. 13, No. 1, pp. 177–183.

Churchilor G. A., & Peter J. (2003). Marketing: creating value for customers. São Paulo: Saraiva.

Clover, V. T. (1950). Relative importance of impulse-buying in retail stores. The Journal of Marketing, Vol. 15, No. 1, pp. 66–70.

Cobb, C. J., & Hoyer, W. D. (1986). Planned versus impulse purchase behavior. Journal of Retailing. Vol. 62, No. 4, pp. 384–409.

Connole, R. J., Benson, J. D., & Khera, I. P. (1977). Cognitive dissonance among innovators. Journal of the Academy of Marketing Science. Vol. 5, No. 1–2, pp. 9–20.

Connor, H., Shaw, S., & Fairhurst, D. (2008). Engaging a new generation of graduates. Education + Training, Vol. 50, No. 5, pp. 366–378.

Constantinides, E. (2004). Influencing the on-line consumer's behavior: the web experience. Internet Research, Vol. 14, No. 2, pp. 111–126.

Cook, D. A., Pallak, M. S., Storms, M. D., & McCaul, K. D. (1976). The effect of forced compliance on attitude change and behavior change. Personality and Social Psychology Bulletin, Vol. 3, No. 1, pp. 71–74.

Cooper, J., Fazio, R. H., & Rhodewalt, F. (1978). Dissonance and humor: Evidence for the undifferentiated nature of dissonance arousal. Journal of Personality and Social Psychology, Vol. 36, No. 3, pp. 280–285.

Costa, F., & Laran, J. (2003). Impulse buying on the internet: antecedents and consequences. In: SMA retail symposium, November.

Costa, P. T. Jr., & McCrae, R. R. (1986). Major contributions to personality psychology. In Modgil, S., and Modgil, C. (eds), Hans Eysenck: Consensus and Controversy. Barcombe Lewes: Falmer, pp. 63–72, 86, 87.

Crawford, J. R., & Henry, J. D. (2004). The Positive and Negative Affect Schedule (PANAS): 707 construct validity, measurement properties and normative data in a large non-clinical 708 sample. British Journal of Clinical Psychology, Vol. 43, pp. 245–265.

Cummings, W. H., & Venkatesan, M. (1976). Cognitive dissonance and consumer behavior: a review of the evidence. Journal of Marketing Research, Vol. 13, No. 3, pp. 303–308.

Das, G., Datta, B., & Guin, K. K. (2012). Impact of retailer personality on consumer-based retailer equity. Asia Pacific Journal of Marketing and Logistics, Vol. 24, No. 4, pp. 619–639.

Davis, F. (1986). Technology Acceptance Model for empirically testing new end-user information systems: theory and results. PhD thesis MIT Sloan School of Management, Cambridge.

REFERENCES 85

Davis, F., Bagozzi, R., & Warshaw, P. (1989). User acceptance of computer technology: a comparison of two theoretical models. Management Science, Vol. 35, No. 8, pp. 982–1003.

Davis, R., & Sajtos, L. (2009). Anytime, anywhere: measuring the ubiquitous consumer's impulse purchase behavior. International Journal of Mobile Marketing, Vol. 4, No. 1, pp. 15–22.

De Hauw, S., & De Vos, A. (2010). Millennials' career perspective and psychological contract expectations: does the recession lead to lowered expectations? Journal of Business and Psychology. Vol. 25, No. 2, pp. 293–302.

de Kervenoael, R., Aykac, D. S. O., & Palmer, M. (2009). On-line social capital: understanding e-impulse buying in practice. Journal of Retailing and Consumer services, Vol. 16, No. 4, pp. 320–328.

Dearing, J. W., & Cox, J. G. (2018). Diffusion of innovations theory, principles, and practice. Health Affairs, Vol. 37, No. 2, pp. 183–190.

Deutsch, R., & Strack, F. (2008). Variants of judgment and decision making: The perspective of the reflective-impulsive model. In H. Plessner, C. Betsch, & T. Betsch (Eds.), Intuition in judgment and decision making (p. 39–53). Lawrence Erlbaum Associates Publishers.

Deutsch, R., Gawronski, B., & Hofmann, W. (Eds.). (2016). Reflective and impulsive determinants of human behavior. Psychology Press, Routledge.

Devine, P. G., Hamilton, D. L. E., & Ostrom, T. M. (1994). Social cognition: impact on social psychology. Academic Press.

Dholakia, U. M. (2000). Temptation and resistance: an integrated model of consumption impulse. Psychol. Mark., 17 (11), pp. 955–982.

Dholakia, R. R., Zhao, M., Dholakia, N., & Fortin, D. R. (2000). Interactivity and revisits to websites: a theoretical framework. Working Paper, RITIM.

Dialogica (2017). Spesa programmata o impulso? I dati di una ricerca. http://dialogica.it/blog/2017/10/26/spesa-programmata-o-impulso-i-dati-di-una-ricerca [Last accessed: June 16, 2020].

Diener, E., Suh, E. M., Lucas, R. E., & Smith, H. L. (1999). Subjective well-being: three decades of progress. Psychological bulletin, Vol. 125, No. 2, pp. 276.

Dimock, M. (2019). Defining generations: where Millennials end and Generation Z begins. Pew Research Center, Vol. 17, pp. 1–7.

Dittmar, H., Beattie, J., & Friese, S. (1995). Gender identity and material symbols: Objects and decision considerations in impulse purchases. Journal of Economic Psychology, Vol. 16, No. 3, pp. 491–511.

Donovan, R. J., Rossiter, J. R., Marcoolyn, G., & Nesdale, A. (1994). Store atmosphere and purchasing behavior. Journal of Retailing, Vol. 70, No. 3, pp. 283–294.

Dreisbach, G. (2006). How positive affect modulates cognitive control: the costs and benefits of reduced maintenance capability. Brain and Cognition, Vol. 60, No. 1, pp. 11–19.

Dreisbach, G., Fischer, R. (2012). Conflicts as aversive signals. Brain and Cognition, 78(2), pp. 94–98.

Duffett, R. G. (2015). Facebook advertising's influence on intention-to-purchase and purchase amongst Millennials. Internet Research. Vol. 24, No. 4, pp. p 498–526

Eastman, J. K., Iyer, R., Liao-Troth, S., Williams, D. F., & Griffin, M. (2014). The role of involvement on millennials' mobile technology behaviors: the moderating impact of status consumption, innovation, and opinion leadership. Journal of Marketing Theory and Practice, Vol. 22, No. 4, pp. 455–470.

Einav, L., Levin, J., Popov, I., & Sundaresan, N. (2014). Growth, adoption, and use of mobile E-commerce. American Economic Review, Vol. 104, No. 5, pp. 489–94.

Eiser, C. (1990). Psychological effects of chronic disease. Journal of Child Psychology and Psychiatry, Vol. 31, No. 1, pp. 85–98.

Elliot, A. J., & Devine, P. G. (1994). On the motivational nature of cognitive dissonance: dissonance as psychological discomfort. Journal of Personality and Social Psychology, Vol. 67, No. 3, pp. 382–394.

eMarketer (2018). Global proximity mobile payment users: eMarketer's estimates for 2016–2021. https://www.emarketer.com/report/global-proximity-mobile-payment-users-emarketers-estimates-20162021/2002187 [Last accessed: July 7, 2020].

eMarketer (2019). US Digital Ad Spending Will Surpass Traditional in 2019, https://www.emarketer.com/content/us-digital-ad-spending-will-surpass-traditional-in-2019 [Last accessed: March 6, 2020].

Engel, J. F., Blackwell, R. D., & Miniard, P. W. (2012). Consumer Behavior, 6th ed. Cengage Learning.

Estrada, C. A., Isen, A. M., & Young, M. J. (1994). Positive affect improves creative problem solving and influences reported source of practice satisfaction in physicians. Motivation and Emotion, Vol. 18, No. 4, pp. 285–299.

Eurostat (2017). Internet purchases by individuals 2008 to 2017 [statistics]. Available from https://ec.europa.eu/eurostat/data/database [Last accessed: March 6, 2020].

Felser, G. (1997). Advertising and consumer psychology: an introduction. Schäffer-Poeschel, Stuttgart.

Festinger, L. (1957). A theory of cognitive dissonance. Stanford University Press.

Festinger, L. (1985). A theory of cognitive dissonance. Stanford University Press, Stanford.

Fishbein, M., & Ajzen, I. (1975). Belief, attitude, intention, and behavior: an introduction to theory and research. Addison-Wesley, Reading, MA.

REFERENCES 87

Flight, R., Roundtree, M., & Beatty, S. (2012). Feeling the urge: Affect in impulsive and compulsive buying. Journal of Marketing Theory and Practice, Vol. 20, Issue 4, 453–466.

Floh, A., & Madlberger, M. (2013). The role of atmospheric cues in on-line impulse-buying behavior. Electronic Commerce Research and Applications, Vol. 12, No. 6, pp. 425–439.

Forman, C., Ghose, A., & Goldfarb, A. (2009). Competition between local and electronic markets: how the benefit of buying on-line depends on where you live. Management Science, Vol. 55, No. 1, pp. 47–57.

Fornell, C., & Larcker, D. F. (1981). Evaluating structural equation models with unobservable variables and measurement error. Journal of Marketing Research, Vol. 18, No. 1, pp. 39–50.

Foxall, G. R. (2002). Consumer behaviour analysis (Vol. 3). Taylor & Francis.

Francis, T., & Hoefel, F. (2018). True Gen: generation Z and its implications for companies. McKinsey & Company.

Fröber, K., & Dreisbach, G. (2012). How positive affect modulates proactive control: reduced usage of informative cues under positive affect with low arousal. Frontiers in Psychology, Vol. 3, No. 1, Art. 265, pp. 1–14.

Fröber, K., & Dreisbach, G. (2014). The differential influences of positive affect, random reward, and performance-contingent reward on cognitive control. Cognitive, Affective, & Behavioral Neuroscience, Vol. 14, No. 2, pp. 530–547.

Furlong, A. (2013). Youth studies: an introduction. New York: Routledge.

Gawronski, B., & Strack, F. (2004). On the propositional nature of cognitive consistency: Dissonance changes explicit, but not implicit attitudes. Journal of Experimental Social Psychology, Vol. 40, No. 4, pp. 535–542.

Gefen, D., & Straub, D. (2000). The relative use of perceived ease of use in IS adoption: a study of e-commerce adoption. Journal of the Association for Information Systems, Vol. 1, No. 8, pp. 1–28.

Gehrt, K. C., Onzo, N., Fujita, K., & Rajan, M. N. (2007). The emergence of internet shopping in Japan: identification of shopping orientation-defined segments. Journal of Marketing Theory and Practice, Vol. 15, No. 2, pp. 167–177.

George, B. P., & Yaoyuneyong, G. (2010). Impulse buying and cognitive dissonance: a study conducted among the spring break student shoppers. Young Consumers. Vol. 11, No. 4, pp. 291–306.

Godin, S. (2018). This is marketing: you can't be seen until you learn to see. Penguin, New York.

Goldenson, R. M. (1984). Longman Dictionary of Psychology and Psychiatry, Kaplan Publishing.

Google Consumer Barometer (2015). The smart shopper: research and purchase behavior (ROPO). Available at https://www.thinkwithgoogle.com/_qs/documents/3520/CB_Country_Report_15_-_France_1.pdf [Last accessed: 7, July 2020].

Goschke, T., & Bolte, A. (2014). Emotional modulation of control dilemmas: the role of positive affect, reward, and dopamine in cognitive stability and flexibility. Neuropsychologia, Vol. 62, pp. 403–423.

Gurau, C. (2012). A life-stage analysis of consumer loyalty profile: comparing generation X and millennial consumers. Journal of Consumer Marketing, Vol. 29, No. 2, pp. 103–113.

Gutfreund, J. (2016). Move over, Millennials: generation Z is changing the consumer landscape. Journal of Brand Strategy, Vol. 5, No. 3, pp. 245–249.

Ha, S. H., Bae, S. M., & Park, S. C. (2002). Customer's time-variant purchase behavior and corresponding marketing strategies: an on-line retailer's case. Computers & Industrial Engineering, Vol. 43, No. 4, pp. 801–820.

Haba, H., Hassan, Z., & Dastane, O. (2017). Factors leading to consumer perceived value of smartphones and its impact on purchase intention. Global Business and Management Research: an International Journal, Vol. 9, No. 1, pp. 42–71.

Harmon-Jones. (2019). Cognitive dissonance: Reexamining a pivotal theory in psychology (pp. 141–157). American Psychological Association.

Harmon-Jones, E., Mills, J. (1999). Cognitive dissonance: progress on a pivotal theory in social psychology. American Psychological Association.

Hartman, J. L., & McCambridge, J. (2011). Optimizing millennials' communication styles. Business Communication Quarterly, Vol. 74, No. 1, pp. 22–44.

Häubl, G., & Trifts, V. (2000). Consumer decision making in on-line shopping environments: the effects of interactive decision aids. Marketing Science, Vol. 19, No. 1, pp. 4–21.

Hausman, A. (2000). A multi-method investigation of consumer motivations in impulse buying behavior. Journal of Consumer Marketing, Vol. 17, No. 5, pp. 403–426.

Hawkins, D. I., & Mothersbaugh, D. L. (2010). Consumer behavior: building marketing strategy. Boston: McGraw-Hill Irwin.

Heilman, C. M., Nakamoto, K., & Rao, A. G. (2002). Pleasant surprises: consumer response to unexpected in-store coupons. Journal of Marketing Research, Vol. 39, No. 2, pp. 242–252.

Hinojosa, A. S., Gardner, W. L., Walker, H. J., Cogliser, C., & Gullifor, D. (2017). A review of cognitive dissonance theory in management research: Opportunities for further development. Journal of Management, 43(1), 170–199.

Hoch, S. J., & Lowenstein, G. F. (1991). Time-inconsistent preferences and consumer self-control. Journal of Consumer Research, Vol. 17, pp. 492–507.

Holloway, R. J. (1967). An experiment on consumer dissonance. Journal of Marketing, Vol. 31, No.1, pp. 39–43.

Howe, N., & Strauss, W. (1992). Generations: The History of America's Future, 1584 to 2069. Perennial, Harper Collins Publishers.

Hoyer, W. D., Macinnis, D. J., & Pieters, R. (2001). Customer behavior. Boston, Houghton Mifflin Company.

Hwang, J., & Griffiths, M. A. (2017). Share more, drive less: millennials value perception and behavioral intent in using collaborative consumption services. Journal of Consumer Marketing. Vol. 32, No. 2, pp. 132–146.

Hwang, W., & Salvendy, G. (2007). What makes evaluators to find more usability problems? A meta-analysis for individual detection rates. In: International conference on human-computer interaction (pp. 499–507). Springer, Berlin, Heidelberg.

Hyman Jr., I. E., Boss, S. M., Wise, B. M., McKenzie, K. E., & Caggiano, J. M. (2010). Did you see the unicycling clown? Inattentional blindness while walking and talking on a cell phone. Applied Cognitive Psychology, Vol. 24, No. 5, pp. 597–607.

Idealo (2018). L'e-commerce in Italia: Le nuove abitudini di acquisto on-line. Available at https://www.idealo.it/magazine/wpcontent/uploads/sites/32/2018/03/2018_ebook_ecommerce_idealo_scarica_gratis_IT.pdf [Last accessed: 7 July, 2020].

Igarashi, T., Takai, J., & Yoshida, T. (2005). Gender differences in social network development via mobile phone text messages: A longitudinal study. Journal of Social and Personal Relationships, Vol. 22, No. 5, pp. 691–713.

Inman, J. J., Winer, R. S., & Ferraro, R. (2009). The interplay among category characteristics, customer characteristics, and customer activities on in-store decision making. Journal of Marketing, 73(5), 19–29.

Iram, M., & Chacharkar, D. Y. (2017). Model of impulse buying behavior. BVIMSR's Journal of Management Research, Vol. 9, No. 1, pp. 45–53.

Iyer, E. S. (1989). Unplanned purchasing: knowledge of shopping environment and Time Pressure. Journal of Retailing, Vol. 65, No. 1, 40–58.

Jeong, M., Zo, H., Lee, C. H., & Ceran, Y. (2019). Feeling displeasure from online social media postings: A study using cognitive dissonance theory. Computers in Human Behavior, 97, 231–240.

Jonas, E., Graupmann, V., & Frey, D. (2006). The influence of mood on the search for supporting versus conflicting information: dissonance reduction as a means of mood regulation? Personality and Social Psychology Bulletin, Vol. 32, No. 1, pp. 3–15.

Jones, C. R., Fazio, R. H., & Olson, M. A. (2009). Implicit misattribution as a mechanism underlying evaluative conditioning. Journal of Personality and Social Psychology, Vol. 96, No. 5, pp. 933–948.

Jones, C., Ramanau, R., Cross, S., & Healing, G. (2010). Net generation or digital natives: is there a distinct new generation entering university? Computers & Education, Vol. 54, No. 3, pp. 722–732.

90 REFERENCES

Jones, E. E., & Kelly, J. R. (2009). No pain, no gains: negative mood leads to process gains in idea-generation groups. Group Dynamics: Theory, Research, and Practice, Vol. 13, No. 2, pp. 75–88.

Jones, M. A., Reynolds, K. E., Weun, S., & Beatty, S. E. (2003). The product-specific nature of impulse buying tendency. Journal of Business Research, Vol. 56, No. 7, pp. 505–511.

Kacen, J. J., & Lee, J. A. (2002). The influence of culture on consumer impulsive buying behavior. Journal of Consumer Psychology, Vol. 12, No. 2, pp. 163–176.

Karjaluoto, H., Karvonen, J., Kesti, M., Koivumäki, T., Manninen, M., Pakola, J., & Salo, J. (2005). Factors affecting consumer choice of mobile phones: two studies from Finland. Journal of Euromarketing, Vol. 14, No. 3, pp. 59–82.

Kim, A. J., & Johnson, K. K. (2016). Power of consumers using social media: examining the influences of brand-related user-generated content on Facebook. Computers in Human Behavior, Vol. 58, pp. 98–108.

Kim, E. Y., & Kim, Y. (2004). Predicting on-line purchase intentions for clothing products. European Journal of Marketing, Vol. 38, No. 7, pp. 883–897.

Kim, S., & Eastin, M. S. (2011). Hedonic tendencies and the on-line consumer: an investigation of the on-line shopping process. Journal of Internet Commerce, Vol. 10, No. 1, pp. 68–90.

Knox, R. E., & Inkster, J. A. (1968). Post-decision dissonance at post time. Journal of Personality and Social Psychology, Vol. 8, No. 4, pp. 319–323.

Kollat, D. T., & Willett, R. P. (1967). Customer impulse purchasing behavior. Journal of Marketing Research, Vol. 4, No. 1, pp. 21–31.

Koller, M., & Salzberger, T. (2007). Cognitive dissonance as a relevant construct throughout the decision-making and consumption process: an empirical investigation related to a package tour. Journal of Customer Behaviour, Vol. 6, N. 3, pp. 217–227.

Korgaonkar, P. K., & Moschis, G. P. (1982). An experimental study of cognitive dissonance, product involvement, expectations, performance and consumer judgement of product performance. Journal of Advertising, Vol. 11, No. 3, pp. 32–44.

Koski, N. (2004). Impulse buying on the internet: encouraging and discouraging factors. Frontiers of E-business Research, Vol. 4, pp. 23–35.

Koufaris, M. (2002). Applying the technology acceptance model and flow theory to on-line consumer behavior. Information Systems Research. Vol. 13, No. 2, pp. 205–223.

Kourouthanassis, P. E., & Giaglis, G. M. (2012). Introduction to the special issue mobile commerce: the past, present, and future of mobile commerce research. International Journal of Electronic Commerce, Vol. 16, No. 4, pp. 5–18.

Kwon, W. S., & Lennon, S. J. (2009). Reciprocal effects between multichannel retailers' offline and on-line brand images. Journal of Retailing, Vol. 85, No. 3, pp. 376–390.

REFERENCES 91

Lai, P. (2017). The literature review of technology adoption models and theories for the novelty technology. Journal of Information Systems and Technology Management, Vol. 14, No. 1, Jan/Apr., 2017 pp. 21–38.

Laird, J. D. (2007). Feelings: The perception of self. Oxford University Press.

Laize, C., & Pougnet, S. (2007). Un modèle de développement des compétences sociales et relationnelles des jeunes d'aujourd'hui et managers de demain. Fribourg: XVIIIème congrès de l'AGRH.

Laurent, G., & Kapferer, J. N. (1985). Measuring consumer involvement profiles. Journal of Marketing Research, Vol. 22, No. 1, pp. 41–53.

Lee, T., Park, C., & Jun, J. (2014). Two faces of mobile shopping: self-efficacy and impulsivity. International Journal of E-business Research. Vol. 10, No. 1, pp. 15–32.

Lenhart, A., Ling, R., Campbell, S., & Purcell, K. (2010). Teens and mobile phones: text messaging explodes as teens embrace it as the centerpiece of their communication strategies with friends. Pew Internet & American Life Project.

Leppaniemi, M., & Karjaluoto, H. (2005). Factors influencing consumers' willingness to accept mobile advertising: a conceptual model. International Journal of Mobile Communications, Vol. 3, No. 3, pp. 197–213.

Levy, M., & Barton, A. (2007). Weitz. Retailing Management. McGraw-Hill Education.

Levy, M., & Weitz, B. A. (2007). Retailing mangement. McGraw-Hill, Irwin.

Li, H., Kuo, C., & Rusell, M. G. (1999). The impact of perceived channel utilities, shopping orientations, and demographics on the consumer's on-line buying behavior. Journal of Computer-Mediated Communication, Vol. 5, No. 2, JCMC521.

Lin, C. P., & Bhattacherjee, A. (2010). Extending technology usage models to interactive hedonic technologies: a theoretical model and empirical test. Information Systems Journal, Vol. 20, No. 2, pp. 163–181.

Lin, C., Chen, C., & Wang, S. (2018). The influence of impulse buying toward consumer loyalty in on-line shopping: a regulatory focus theory perspective. Journal of Ambient Intelligence and Humanized Computing, Vol. 9, No. 4, pp. 1–11.

Losch, M. E., & Cacioppo, J. T. (1990). Cognitive dissonance may enhance sympathetic tonus, but attitudes are changed to reduce negative affect rather than arousal. Journal of Experimental Social Psychology. Vol. 26, No. 4, pp. 289–304.

Luna, R., & Quintanilla, I. (2000). El modelo de compra ACB. Una nueva conceptualizacion de la compra por impulso. Esic Market. Revista Internacional de Economía y Empresa, Vol. 106, No.1, pp. 151–163.

Mack, Z., & Sharples, S. (2009). The importance of usability in product choice: a mobile phone case study. Ergonomics, Vol. 52, No. 12, pp. 1514–1528.

Malester, J. (2006). TWICE: this week in consumer electronics. Consumer Electronics, Vol. 21, No. 10, p. 104.

Mallalieu, L., & Palan, K. M. (2006). How good a shopper am I? Conceptualizing teenage girls' perceived shopping competence. Academy of Marketing Science Review, Vol, 2005, No. 5, Available: http://www.amsreview.org/article/mallalieu05-2006.pdf.

Mangold, W. G., & Smith, K. T. (2012). Selling to Millennials with on-line reviews. Business Horizons, Vol. 55, No. 2, pp. 141–153.

Maniar, N., Bennett, E., Hand, S., & Allan, G. (2008). The effect of mobile phone screen size on video-based learning. Journal of Software, Vol. 3, No. 4, pp. 51–61.

Mauss, I. B., & Robinson, M. D. (2009). Measures of emotion: a review. Cognition and Emotion, Vol. 23, No. 2, pp. 209–237.

Mayer, J. D., Gaschke, Y. N., Braverman, D. L., & Evans, T. W. (1992). Mood-congruent judgment is a general effect. Journal of Personality and Social Psychology, Vol. 63, No. 1, pp. 119–132.

Mayer, R. E. (1992). Thinking, problem solving, cognition. WH Freeman/Times Books/Henry Holt & Co.

Mayer, R. E. (2005). Cognitive theory of multimedia learning. In R. E. Mayer (Ed.), The Cambridge Handbook of Multimedia Learning (pp. 31–48). New York: Cambridge University Press.

McCloskey, D. (2004). Evaluating electronic commerce acceptance with the technology acceptance model. Journal of Computer Information Systems, Vol. 44, No. 2, pp. 49–57.

McHaney, R. (2012). The new digital shoreline: how Web 2.0 and millennials are revolutionizing higher education. Stylus Publishing, LLC.

McKnight, D. H., Choudhury, V., & Kacmar, C. (2002). Developing and validating trust measures for e-commerce: An integrative typology. Information Systems Research, Vol. 13, No. 3, pp. 334–359.

Merz, E. L., Malcarne, V. L., Roesch, S. C., Ko, C. M., Emerson, M., Roma, V. G., & Sadler, G. R. (2013). Psychometric properties of Positive and Negative Affect Schedule (PANAS) original and short forms in an African American community sample. Journal of Affective Disorders, Vol. 151, No. 3, pp. 942–949.

Mills, J. (2019). Improving the 1957 version of dissonance theory. In E. Harmon-Jones (Ed.), Cognitive dissonance: Reexamining a pivotal theory in psychology (p. 27–39). American Psychological Association.

Mirsch, T., Lehrer, C., & Jung, R. (2016). Channel integration towards omnichannel management: a literature review. Conference: Pacific Asia Conference on Information Systems (PACIS). At: Chiayi, Taiwan.

Mittal, B. (1989). A Theoretical analysis of two recent measures of involvement. Advances in Consumer Research, 16(1).

REFERENCES   93

Mohan, G., Sharina, P., & Sivakumaran, B. (2013). Impact of store environment on impulse buying behavior. European Journal of Marketing, Vol. 47, No. 10, pp. 1711–1732.

Mowen, J. C., & Minor, M. (1995). Customer behavior. New Jersey: Prentice Hall Inc.

Murray, K. B., & Häubl, G. (2008). Interactive consumer decision aids. In: Wierenga, B., Handbook of marketing decision models. New York, NY: Springer Science & Business Media, LLC.

Nielsen (2016). Millennials are top smartphone users. http://www.nielsen.com/us/en/insights/news/2016/millennials-are-top-smartphone-users.html [Last accessed June 16, 2020].

Noble, S. M., Haytko, D. L., & Phillips, J. (2009). What drives college-age generation Y consumers? Journal of Business Research, Vol. 62, No. 1, pp. 617–628.

Novak, T. P., Hoffman, D. L., & Yung, Y. F. (1998). Modeling the Structure of the Flow Experience. Informs Marketing Science and the Internet Mini-Conference.

Novak, T. P., Hoffman, D. L., & Yung, Y. (2000). Measuring the customer experience in on-line environments: a structural modeling approach. Marketing Science, Vol. 19, No. 1, pp. 22–42.

Nunes, J. C., & Drèze, X. (2006). The endowed progress effect: how artificial advancement increases effort. Journal of Consumer Research, Vol. 32, No. 4, pp. 504–512.

Nunnally, J. C. (1978). Psychometric theory. McGraw-Hill, New York, 2nd Edition.

O'Guinn, T. C., & Faber, R. J. (1989). Compulsive buying: a phenomenological exploration. Journal of Consumer Research, Vol. 16, pp. 147–157.

Okazaki, S., & Mendez, F. (2013). Exploring convenience in mobile commerce: Moderating effects of gender. Computers in Human Behavior, Vol. 29, No. 3, pp. 1234–1242.

Oliver, R.L. (1997). Satisfaction: a behavioral perspective on the consumer. Boston: McGraw-Hill.

Ordun, G. (2015). Millennial (Gen Y) consumer behavior their shopping preferences and perceptual maps associated with brand loyalty. Canadian Social Science, Vol. 11, No. 4, pp. 40–55.

Pallak, M. S., & Kiesler, C. A. (1968). Dissonance arousal, task evaluation, and task performance. Psychonomic Science, Vol. 11, No. 6, pp. 197–198.

Park, C. W., MacInnis, D. J., & Priester, J. R. (2006). Beyond attitudes: attachment and consumer behavior. Seoul National Journal, Vol. 12, No. 2, pp. 3–36.

Park, E. J., & Forney, J. C. (2004). A comparison of impulse buying behavior and credit card use between Korean and American college students. Journal of the Korean Society of Clothing and Textiles, Vol. 28, No. 12, pp. 1571–1582.

94 REFERENCES

Peck, J., & Childers, T. L. (2006). If I touch it, I have to have it: individual and environmental influences on impulse purchasing. Journal of Business Research, Vol. 59, No. 6, pp. 765–769.

Pepels, W. (2005). Käuferverhalten: Basiswissen für Kaufentscheidungen von Konsumenten und Organisationen; mit Aufgaben und Lösungen. Erich Schmidt.

Petty, R. E., & Cacioppo, J. T. (1996). Attitudes and persuasion: classic and contemporary approaches. Westview Press.

Petty, R. E., & Cacioppo, J. T. (1986). The elaboration likelihood model of persuasion. In: Berkowitz, L., editor. Advances in Experimental Social Psychology (vol. XIX). New York: Academic Press.

Phau, I., & Lo, C. C. (2004). Profiling fashion innovators. Journal of Fashion Marketing and Management: an International Journal. Vol. 8, No. 4, pp. 399–411.

Pirog, S. F., & Roberts, J. A. (2007). Personality and credit card misuse among college students: the mediating role of impulsiveness. Journal of Marketing Theory and Practice, Vol. 15, No. 1, pp. 65–77.

Piron, F. (1991). Defining impulse purchasing. ACR North American Advances.

Piron, F. (1993). A comparison of emotional reactions experienced by planned, unplanned and impulse purchasers. in NA - Advances in Consumer Research Volume 20, eds. Leigh McAlister and Michael L. Rothschild, Provo, UT: Association for Consumer Research, pp. 341–344.

Pittman, T. S. (1975). Attribution of arousal as mediator in dissonance reduction. Journal of Experimental Social Psychology. Vol. 11, No. 1, pp. 53–63.

Podoshen, J. S., & Andrzejewski, S. A. (2012). An examination of the relationships between materialism, conspicuous consumption, impulse buying, and brand loyalty. Journal of Marketing Theory and Practice, Vol. 20, No. 3, pp. 319–334.

Rackspace (2012), Tablets and smartphones may increase UK consumer impulse buys by up to £1.1 billion per year, indicates Rackspace retail research. https://www.rackspace.com/en-gb/newsroom/tablets-smartphones-may-increase-uk-consumer-impulse-buys-1-1-billion-per-year-indicates-rackspace-retail-research [Last accessed: March 15, 2020].

Raines, C. (2002). Managing millennials. Connecting Generations: The Sourcebook.

Rogers, E.M. (1962). Diffusion of innovation. New York: Free Press of Glencoe.

Rook, D. W. (1987). The Buying Impulse. Journal of Consumer Research, Vol. 14, No. 2, pp. 189–197.

Rook, D. W., & Fisher, R. J. (1995). Normative influences on impulsive buying behavior. Journal of Consumer Research, Vol. 22, No. 3, pp. 305–313.

Rook, D. W., & Hoch, S. J. (1985). Consuming impulses. Advances in Consumer Research, Vol. 12, No. 1, pp. 23–27.

Rose, R. (2001). On the negative effects of e-commerce: a socio-cognitive exploration of unregulated on-line buying. Journal of Computer-mediated Communication, Vol. 6, No. 3, JCMC631.

Rose, S., Hair, N., & Clark, M. (2011). On-line customer experience: a review of the business-to-consumer on-line purchase context. International Journal of Management Reviews, Vol. 13, No. 1, pp. 24–39.

Rowe, G., Hirsh, J. B., & Anderson, A. K. (2007). Positive affect increases the breadth of attentional selection. Proceedings of the national academy of sciences, Vol. 104, No. 1, pp. 383–388.

Rush, J., & Hofer, S. M. (2014). Differences in Within- and Between-Person Factor Structure of Positive and Negative Affect: Analysis of Two Intensive Measurement Studies Using Multilevel Structural Equation Modeling. Psychological Assessment, 26(2).

Saif, S. M., & Wahid, A. (2017). Effort estimation techniques for web application development: a review. International Journal of Advanced Research in Computer Science, Vol. 8, No. 9, pp. 125–131.

Sánchez-Martínez, M., & Otero, A. (2009). Factors associated with cell phone use in adolescents in the community of Madrid (Spain). Cyber Psychology & Behavior, Vol. 12, No. 2, pp. 131–137.

Santini, F. D. O., Ladeira, W. J., Vieira, V. A., Araujo, C. F., & Sampaio, C. H. (2019). Antecedents and consequences of impulse buying: a meta-analytic study. RAUSP Management Journal, Vol. 54, No. 2, pp. 178–204.

Schwarz, N. (1990). Feelings as information: informational and motivational functions of affective states. In: Higgins, E.T., Sorrentino, R., (eds): Handbook of motivation and cognition: foundations of social behavior, Vol. 2. Guilford Press, pp. 527–561.

Sciandra, M., & Inman, J. (2013). Smart phones, bad decisions? The impact of in-store mobile technology use on consumer decisions. in NA - Advances in Consumer Research Vol. 41, eds. Simona Botti and Aparna Labroo, Duluth, MN: Association for Consumer Research.

Seock, Y. K. (2003). Analysis of clothing websites for young customer retention based on a model of customer relationship management via the internet (Doctoral dissertation, Virginia Tech).

Shah, M., Guha, S., & Shrivastava, U. (2012). Effect of emerging trends in retail sector on impulse buying behavior. International Journal of Ems, Vol. 3, No. 2.

Shankar, V., Hofacker, C., Venkatesh, A., & Naik, P. (2010). Mobile Marketing in the Retailing Environment: Current Insights and Future Research Avenues. Journal of Interactive Marketing, 24(2), pp. 111–120.

Sharma, P., Sivakumaran, B., & Marshall, R. (2010). Exploring impulse buying and variety seeking by retail shoppers: towards a common conceptual framework. Journal of Marketing Management, Vol. 26, No. 5–6, pp. 473–494.

Shin, C., Hong, J. H., & Dey, A. K. (2012). Understanding and prediction of mobile application usage for smart phones. In: Proceedings of the 2012 ACM Conference on Ubiquitous Computing, pp. 173–182.

Simon, B., Bildungssektor, W., & Akzeptanzuntersuchung an Hochschulen, E. (2001). Knowledge media in the education system: acceptance research in universities. In W. V. Business. Vienna, Austria.

Simonson, I. (1990). The effect of purchase quantity and timing on variety-seeking behavior. Journal of Marketing Research, Vol. 27, No. 2, pp. 150–162.

Simpson, B., & Willer, R. (2008). Altruism and indirect reciprocity: the interaction of person and situation in prosocial behavior. Social Psychology Quarterly, Vol. 71, No. 1, pp. 37–52.

Sinclair, R. C., Mark, M. M., & Clore, G. L. (1994). Mood-related persuasion depends on (mis) attributions. Social Cognition, Vol. 12, No. 4, pp. 309–326.

Slickdeals (2018). Slickdeals shares new survey data showing Americans spend $324,000 on impulse buys in their lifetime. https://slickdeals.net/forums/forumdisplay.php?f=39 [Last accessed: June 16, 2020].

Smith, J. R., Terry, D. J., Manstead, A. S., Louis, W. R., Kotterman, D., & Wolfs, J. (2008). The attitude–behavior relationship in consumer conduct: The role of norms, past behavior, and self-identity. The Journal of Social Psychology, Vol. 148, No. 3, pp. 311–334.

Sofi, S. A., & Najar, S. A. (2018). Impact of personality influencers on psychological paradigms: an empirical discourse of big five framework and impulsive buying behaviour. European Research on Management and Business Economics, Vol. 24, No. 2, pp. 71–81.

Sopadjieva, E., Dholakia, U.M., & Benjamin, B. (2017). A Study of 46,000 Shoppers Shows That Omnichannel Retailing Works. Harvard Business Review, January 03.

Soto-Acosta, P., Molina-Castillo, F. J., Lopez-Nicolas, C., & Colomo-Palacios, R. (2014). The effect of information overload and disorganisation on intention to purchase on-line: the role of perceived risk and internet experience. On-line Information Review, Vol. 38 No. 4, pp. 543–561.

Srivastava, L. (2005). Mobile phones and the evolution of social behaviour. Behaviour & Information Technology, pp. 111–129.

Stern, H. (1962). The significance of impulse buying today. Journal of Marketing, Vol. 26, No. 2, pp. 59–62.

Stewart, J. S., Oliver, E. G., Cravens, K. S., & Oishi, S. (2017). Managing millennials: embracing generational differences. Business Horizons, Vol. 60, No. 1, pp. 45–54.

Stone, J., & Cooper, J. (2001). A self-standards model of cognitive dissonance. Journal of Experimental Social Psychology, 37(3), pp. 228–243.

Stone, R., Cooper, S., & Cant, R. (2013). The value of peer learning in undergraduate nursing education: A systematic review. ISRN nursing, 2013.

REFERENCES   97

Sun, T., & Wu, G. (2011). Trait predictors of on-line impulsive buying tendency: A hierarchical approach. Journal of Marketing Theory and Practice, Vol. 19, No. 3, pp. 337–346.

Sundström, M., Balkow, J., Florhed, J., Tjernström, M., & Wadenfors, P. (2013). Inpulsive buying behaviour: the role of feelings when shopping for on-line fashion. In: 17th European association for education and research in commercial distribution.

Sweeney, J. C. (2000). Cognitive dissonance after purchase: a multidimensional scale. Psychology & Marketing, Vol.17, No. 5, pp. 369–385.

Sweeney, J., & Chew, M. (2000). Consumer-brand relationships: an exploratory study in the services context. In: Consumer-brand relationships: an exploratory study in the services context (pp. 1234–1238). Promaco Conventions Pty. Ltd.

Taherdoost, H. (2018). A review of technology acceptance and adoption models and theories. Procedia Manufacturing, 22, 961.

Tellegen, A. (1982). Brief manual for the multidimensional personality questionnaire. Unpublished manuscript, University of Minnesota, Minneapolis, pp. 1031–1010.

Tifferet, S., & Herstein, R. (2012). Gender differences in brand commitment, impulse buying, and hedonic consumption. Journal of Product & Brand Management., Vol. 21, No. 3, pp. 176–182.

Troilo, G. (2015). Marketing in creative industries: value, experience and creativity. Macmillan International Higher Education.

Turner, A. (2015). Generation Z: technology and social interest. The Journal of Individual Psychology, 71(2), 103–113.

Twenge, J. (2006). Generation me: why today's young Americans are more confident, assertive, entitled – and more miserable than ever before. New York: Free Press Simon and Schuster.

UPS (2016). UPS Pulse of the On-line Shopper. Available at https://pressroom.ups.com/assets/pdf/2016_UPS_Pulse%20of%20the%20On-line%20Shopper_executive%20summary_final.pdf [Last accessed: June 16, 2020].

van der Heijden, H. (2004). User acceptance of hedonic information systems. MIS Quarterly (28:4), pp. 695–704.

van der Heijden, H., Verhagen, T., & Creemers, M. (2003). Understanding on-line purchase intentions: contributions from technology and trust perspectives. European Journal of Information Systems, Vol. 12, pp. 41–48.

van Wouwe, N. C., Band, G. P., & Ridderinkhof, K. R. (2011). Positive affect modulates flexibility and evaluative control. Journal of Cognitive Neuroscience, Vol. 23, No. 3, pp. 524–539.

Venkatesh, V., & Bala, H. (2008). Technology acceptance model 3 and a research agenda on interventions. Decision Sciences, Vol. 39, No. 2, pp. 273–315.

Venkatesh, V., & Davis, F. D. (2000). A theoretical extension of the technology acceptance model: four longitudinal field studies. Management Science, Vol. 46, No. 2, pp. 186–204.

Venkatesh, V., Morris, M. G., Davis G. B., & Davi, F. D. (2003). User acceptance of information technology: towards a unified view. MIS Quarterly, pp. 425–478.

Venkatesh, V., Thong, J., & Xu, X. (2012). Consumer acceptance and use of information technology: extending the unified theory of acceptance and use of technology. MIS Quarterly, pp. 161.

Venkatraman, V., & Huettel, S. A. (2012). Strategic control in decision-making under uncertainty. European Journal of Neuroscience, Vol. 35, No. 7, pp. 1075–1082.

Verplanken, B., & Herabadi, A. (2001). Individual differences in impulse buying tendency: feeling and no thinking. European Journal of Personality, Vol. 15(S1), pp. S71–S83.

Verplanken, B., Herabadi, A. G., Perry, J. A., & Silvera, D. H. (2005). Consumer style and health: the role of impulsive buying in unhealthy eating. Psychology and Health, Vol. 20, No. 4, pp. 429–441.

Verton, D. (2001). Not so happy holiday on-line. Computerworld, Vol. 35, No. 1, pp. 1–15.

Vijayasarathy, L. R., & Jones, J. M. (2000). Intentions to shop using internet catalogues: exploring the effects of product types, shopping orientations, and attitudes towards computers. Electronic Markets, Vol. 10, No. 1, pp. 29–38.

Vodanovich, S., Sundaram, D., & Myers, M. (2010). Research commentary-digital natives and ubiquitous information systems. Information Systems Research, Vol. 21, No. 4, pp. 711–723.

Wang, Z., Singh, S. N., Li, Y. J., Mishra, S., Ambrose, M., & Biernat, M. (2017). Effects of employees' positive affective displays on customer loyalty intentions: an emotions as social information perspective. Academy of Management Journal, Vol. 60, No. 1, pp. 109–129.

Ward, S., & Wackman, D. B. (1972). Children's purchase influence attempts and parental yielding. Journal of Marketing Research, Vol. 9, No. 3, pp. 316–319.

Watson, D., & Clark, L. A. (1984). Negative affectivity: the disposition to experience aversive emotional states. Psychological Bulletin, Vol. 96, No. 3, pp. 465.

Watson, D., Clark, L. A., & Tellegen, A. (1988). Development and validation of brief measures of positive and negative affect: the PANAS scales. Journal of Personality and Social Psychology, Vol. 54, No. 6, pp. 1063–1070.

Weideli, D. (2013). Environmental analysis of US on-line shopping. Journal of Consumer Research, Vol.12, pp. 29–43.

Weinberg, P., & Gottwald, W. (1982). Impulsive consumer buying as a result of emotions. Journal of Business Research, Vol. 10, No. 1, pp. 43–57.

Wellman, B., Boase, J., & Chen, W. (2002). The networked nature of community: on-line and offline. It & Society, Vol. 1, No. 1, pp. 151–165.

REFERENCES 99

Williams, A. (2015). Move over, millennials, here comes Generation Z. The New York Times, Vol. 18.

Wong, K. (2018). Top 5 trends driving e-commerce: influential takeaways from the report retailers cannot ignore. Journal of Consumer Research, Vol. 72, No. 1, pp.13–42.

Wood, M. (2005). Discretionary unplanned buying in consumer society. Journal of Consumer Behavior, Vol. 4, pp. 268–281.

Xiang, L., Zheng, X., Lee, M. K., & Zhao, D. (2016). Exploring consumers' impulse buying behavior on social commerce platform: the role of parasocial interaction. International Journal of Information Management, Vol. 36, No. 3, pp. 333–347.

Xiao, S. H., & Nicholson, M. (2013). A multidisciplinary cognitive behavioural framework of impulse buying: a systematic review of the literature. International Journal of Management Reviews, Vol. 15, No. 3, pp. 333–356.

Xue, S., Cui, J., Wang, K., Zhang, S., Qiu, J., & Luo, Y. (2013). Positive emotion modulates cognitive control: an event-related potentials study. Scandinavian Journal of Psychology, Vol. 54, No. 2, pp. 82–88.

Yang, S., & Ghose, A. (2010). Analyzing the relationship between organic and sponsored search advertising: positive, negative, or zero interdependence? Marketing Science, Vol. 29, No. 4, pp. 602–623.

Youn, S., & Faber, R. J. (2000). Impulse buying: its relation to personality traits and cues. Advances in Consumer Research, Vol. 27, No. 1, pp. 179–185.

Yu, C., & Bastin, M. (2010). Hedonic shopping value and impulse buying behavior in transitional economies: a symbiosis in the Mainland China marketplace. Journal of Brand Management, Vol. 18, No. 2, pp. 105–114.

Zaichkowsky, J. L. (1985). Measuring the involvement construct. Journal of Consumer Research, Vol. 12, No. 3, pp. 341–352.

Zanna, M. P., & Aziza, C. (1976). On the interaction of repression-sensitization and attention in resolving cognitive dissonance. Journal of Personality, Vol. 44, No. 4, pp. 577–593.

Zanna, M. P., & Cooper, J. (1974). Dissonance and the pill: an attribution approach to studying the arousal properties of dissonance. Journal of Personality and Social Psychology, Vol. 29, No. 5, pp. 703–709.

Zevon, M. A., & Tellegen, A. (1982). The structure of mood change: An idiographic/nomothetic analysis. Journal of Personality and Social Psychology, Vol. 43, No. 1, pp. 111–122.

CPSIA information can be obtained
at www.ICGtesting.com
Printed in the USA
LVHW031112210221
679567LV00004B/219